Standard Grade | Foundation | General

English

Leckie x Leckie

First exam published in 2004.
Published by Leckie & Leckie Ltd, 3rd Floor, 4 Queen Street, Edinburgh EH2 1JE
tel: 0131 220 6831 fax: 0131 225 9987 enquiries@leckieandleckie.co.uk www.leckieandleckie.co.uk

ISBN 978-1-84372-628-9

A CIP Catalogue record for this book is available from the British Library.

Leckie & Leckie is a division of Huveaux plc.

Leckie & Leckie is grateful to the copyright holders, as credited at the back of the book, for permission to use their material.
Every effort has been made to trace the copyright holders and to obtain their permission for the use of copyright material.
Leckie & Leckie will gladly receive information enabling them to rectify any error or omission in subsequent editions.

[BLANK PAGE]

F

0860/401

NATIONAL
QUALIFICATIONS
2004

WEDNESDAY, 5 MAY
10.35 AM – 11.25 AM

**ENGLISH
STANDARD GRADE**
Foundation Level
Reading
Text

Read carefully the passage overleaf. It will help if you read it twice. When you have done so, answer the questions. Use the spaces provided in the Question/Answer booklet.

SCOTTISH
QUALIFICATIONS
AUTHORITY

In this extract the narrator and his brother are on an overnight camping and hunting trip when something unusual happens.

1   At some point I drifted off to sleep and when I woke I thought it was dawn. Then I realised the pale light coming through the canvas was moonlight. I was absolutely alert, and tense. Something had wakened me. I lay there, hardly daring to breathe. Then I heard a whisper, a low hiss of a whisper, outside the tent. It was calling my name.

2   Somebody was out there. My brother was breathing gently beside me, fast asleep. I simply listened. I don't know what I thought. I felt no fear, but still I was amazed to feel the tears trickling slowly down over my ears, as I lay staring upwards.

3   The whisper came again, my name. It seemed to be coming from about where the fire was.

4   Very carefully, partly not to waken my brother, partly not to let the voice know I was listening, I sat up, leaned forward, and tried to peep through the laced-up door of the tent. By holding the edges of the flaps slightly apart, I could see a tiny dot of red glow still in our campfire. Everything out there was drenched in a grey, misty light.

5   Somebody was standing beside the fire.

6   It was a person and yet I got the impression it was somehow not a person. Or it was a very small person. It looked like a small old woman, with a peculiar bonnet on her head and a long shawl. That was my impression. As I stared with all my might, trying to make out something definite, this figure drifted backwards into the shade of the trees. But the whisper came again:

7   "Come out. Quickly. There's been an accident."

8   I immediately knew it must be somebody from the farm. Surely it was the farmer's little old mother. That was how she knew we were here. The farmer had fallen down a well, or down a loft ladder, or a mad cow had crushed his ribs. Or he'd simply tumbled downstairs going to get his old mother a cup of tea because she couldn't sleep.

9   Something stopped me waking my brother. What I really wanted was to find out more. Who was this person? What was the accident? Anyway, it was my name that had been called. It must be me that was specially needed. I could come back and tell my brother later. Most of all, I wanted to see who this was.

10   I had gone to sleep in my clothes, to keep warm and for a quick start. So now I pulled on my boots. I unlaced the tent door at the bottom and crawled out. The grass was cold and soaking under my hands.

11   "Hurry," came the whisper from under the trees. "Hurry, hurry."

12   It seems strange, that I felt no fear. I was so sure that it was somebody from the farm, that I thought of no other possibility. Only huge curiosity, and excitement. Also, I felt quite important suddenly.

13   I went toward the voice, staring into the dark shade. The moon was past full but very hard and white. I wanted to get into the shade quickly, where I wouldn't be so visible.

14   But now the voice came again, from further up the wood. Yes, the voice was climbing towards the farm.

15   "Hurry," it kept saying. "Hurry up."

16   Beneath the trees, the slope was clear and grassy, without brambles or under-growth. Easy going but steep, with that tough, slippery grass.

17   As I climbed, the voice went ahead. Very soon, I would see through the top of the wood. The bright night sky was piled with brilliant masses of snowy cloud, beyond the dark tree stems. I glimpsed the black outline now and again, the funny bonnet, climbing ahead, bobbing between the trees.

18   "Are you coming?" came the whisper again. "This way."

19   I saw her shape in the gap of the wall, clear against those snowy clouds. Then she had gone through it. It was now, as I came up towards the gap, sometimes grasping grass to help myself upwards, that I saw something else, bouncing and scrabbling under the wall, in a clear patch of moonlight.

20   A great slab of stone had fallen. Beside it sat a well-grown fox cub, staring up at me, panting. As I took this in, the cub suddenly started again, tugging and bouncing, jerking and scrabbling, without a sound, till again it crouched there, staring up at me, its mouth wide open, its tongue dangling, panting.

21   I could see now that it was trapped by one hind leg and its tail. They were pinned to the ground under the corner of the big slab.

22   The smell was overpowering, thick, choking, almost liquid, as if concentrated liquid scent had been poured over me, soaking my clothes and hands. I knew the smell of fox – the smell of frightened fox.

23   Then I looked up and saw the figure out there in the field, only five yards away, watching me. More than ever I could see it was a little old woman, with her very thin legs and her funny bonnet and shawl. She did not seem to be wanting me to go to the farm. She had brought me to this fox cub. She was probably some eccentric old lady who never slept, or slept only by day and spent the night roaming the hillsides, talking to owls and befriending foxes. She would have seen our camp. Probably some of those tracks had been hers, brushed through the dew around our tent. Now she had found the trapped cub, and not being strong enough to lift the slab, she had come to us. She wanted me to lift the slab and free the cub. She had not called my brother because she thought he might kill it. She must have watched us, and heard him speak my name.

24   My first thought was to catch the cub and keep it alive. But how could I hold it and at the same time lift the slab? It was a desperate, ferocious little thing. I could have wrapped it in my jersey, knotting the arms round it. But I didn't think of that. As I put my fingers under the other corner of the slab, the cub snapped its teeth at me and hissed like a cat, then struggled again, jerking to free itself.

25   With all my strength I was just able to budge the slab a fraction. But it was enough. As the slab shifted, the cub scrabbled and was gone – off down the wood like a rocket.

26   I looked up at the old lady, and this was my next surprise. The bare, close-cropped, moonlit field was empty. I walked out to where she had been. The whole wide field, under the great bare sky of moonlight, all made much brighter by that great bulging heap of snowy, silvery clouds, was empty. Not even a sheep. Absolutely nothing.

Adapted from *Deadfall* by Ted Hughes

[*END OF PASSAGE*]

[BLANK PAGE]

FOR OFFICIAL USE

F

Total
Mark

0860/402

NATIONAL
QUALIFICATIONS
2004

WEDNESDAY, 5 MAY
10.35 AM – 11.25 AM

ENGLISH
STANDARD GRADE
Foundation Level
Reading
Questions

Fill in these boxes and read what is printed below.

Full name of centre

Town

Forename(s)

Surname

Date of birth
Day   Month   Year

Scottish candidate number

Number of seat

NB Before leaving the examination room you must give this booklet to the invigilator.
If you do not, you may lose all the marks for this paper.

SCOTTISH
QUALIFICATIONS
AUTHORITY

Marks

QUESTIONS

Write your answers in the spaces provided.

Look at Paragraph 1.

1. **Write down an expression** which shows that the boy was unsure of when he had fallen asleep.

   _____   2 ■ 0

2. What made the boy think that he had slept until dawn?

   _____   2 ■ 0

3. What did the boy hear and what was unusual about it?

   _____   2 1 0

4. **Write down two expressions** from Paragraph 1 which show how the boy was feeling.   2 1 0

   (i) _____

   (ii) _____

Look at Paragraphs 2 and 3.

5. "Somebody was out there." (Paragraph 2)

   Why does the writer use this short sentence here?

   _____

   _____   2 1 0

6. Why was the boy's brother unaware of what was happening?

   _____   2 ■ 0

Look at Paragraph 4.

7. **Write down two reasons** why the boy moved very carefully inside the tent.   2 1 0

   (i) _____

   (ii) _____

PAGE TOTAL

Marks

8. What was **the first thing** the boy saw when he peeped through the tent flap?

_____ 2 1 0

9. "Everything out there was drenched in a grey, misty light."

Why does the writer use the word "drenched"?

_____

_____ 2 1 0

Look at Paragraphs 5 to 8.

10. **Write down three things** the boy noticed about the person standing beside the fire. 2 1 0

(i) _____

(ii) _____

(iii) _____

11. **Write down an expression** from Paragraph 6 which tells you that the boy was concentrating on the figure.

_____ 2 ■ 0

12. What important information did the figure give to the boy?

_____ 2 ■ 0

Look at Paragraphs 9 to 11.

13. **Write down three reasons** the boy gives for not wakening his brother. 2 1 0

(i) _____

(ii) _____

(iii) _____

14. Why was it possible for the boy to get ready so quickly?

_____ 2 ■ 0

PAGE
TOTAL

Marks

Look at Paragraphs 12 to 14.

15. **Write down two expressions** which tell you the boy was certain that it was someone from the farm.

2 | 1 | 0

(i) _____

(ii) _____

16. **In your own words** what reason does the boy give for getting into the shade quickly?

_____

_____

2 | 1 | 0

Look at Paragraphs 15 to 18.

17. **Write down an expression** which helps to make the meaning of "glimpsed" clear.

_____

2 | ■ | 0

Look at Paragraphs 19 to 22.

18. In what **two different ways** does the writer make the trapped fox cub's panic clear in Paragraph 20?

2 | 1 | 0

(i) _____

(ii) _____

19. **In your own words** what was the boy's reaction to the smell of the fox?

_____

_____

2 | 1 | 0

Look at Paragraph 23.

20. What did the boy now realise about the little old lady's purpose in leading him there?

_____

2 | ■ | 0

21. **Write down the word** from Paragraph 23 which the boy uses to describe the little old lady's odd behaviour.

_____

2 | ■ | 0

PAGE
TOTAL

Marks

22. Write down two reasons why she had chosen the boy to rescue the cub.

(i) _____

(ii) _____

2 1 0

Look at Paragraphs 24 to 26.

23. ". . . ferocious little thing." (Paragraph 24)

Write down two expressions from later in the paragraph which develop this idea.

(i) _____

(ii) _____

2 1 0

24. Why does the writer use the expression "off down the wood like a rocket" to describe the cub's movements?

_____

_____

2 1 0

Think about the passage as a whole.

25. Who do you think the old lady was? **Using evidence from the passage** give a reason for your answer.

_____

_____

_____

2 1 0

[END OF QUESTION PAPER]

PAGE
TOTAL

FOR OFFICIAL USE

p2 ☐

p3 ☐

p4 ☐

p5 ☐

TOTAL
MARK ☐

[BLANK PAGE]

G

0860/403

NATIONAL
QUALIFICATIONS
2004

WEDNESDAY, 5 MAY
1.00 PM – 1.50 PM

ENGLISH
STANDARD GRADE
General Level
Reading
Text

Read carefully the passage overleaf. It will help if you read it twice. When you have done so, answer the questions. Use the spaces provided in the Question/Answer booklet.

SCOTTISH
QUALIFICATIONS
AUTHORITY

Pucker Way to Kiss a Hummingbird

Mark Carwardine puts on lipstick in Arizona for a wild encounter.

1   There's a rather embarrassing tradition in wildlife circles in certain parts of Arizona. Visiting naturalists are encouraged to try to "kiss" a wild hummingbird.

2   This is more of a challenge for men than it is for women – mainly because it involves wearing lots of red lipstick. A dress and high heels are optional, but the redder and thicker the lipstick the better. Hummingbirds drink nectar from flowers that are often bright red and have learned to associate this particular colour with food. They mistake your mouth for one of their favourite plants – at least, that's the theory.

3   Which is how I found myself high in the mountains of South-East Arizona, with puckered lips pointing sky-ward and a crowd of bemused onlookers egging me on.

4   My home for a couple of days was Beatty's Guest Ranch near the Mexico border. Run by Tom and Edith Beatty, the ranch is nearly 6,000ft above sea level, nestling between two enormous peaks, with spectacular views down the valley to the desert below.

5   According to the South-Eastern Arizona Bird Observatory, it is the hottest hummingbird-watching spot in the state. Thousands of "hummers" arrive in April and May and stay until early October. No fewer than 15 different species are found here on a regular basis.

6   Dozens of special hummingbird feeders, looking like upside-down jam jars, are dotted around the ranch. Hanging from trees, bushes, fences and buildings they are full of a simple magic potion (four parts water, one part white sugar) similar to the nectar of hummingbird flowers. Tom and Edith keep the feeders topped up, getting through a mind-boggling 550 2lb bags of sugar in a typical year.

7   There were two feeders outside my

SUMMER SPECTACLE:
Thousands of hummingbirds arrive in Arizona every year

bedroom window in the turn-of-the-century self-catering cabin on the forest edge (not a good place to stay if you've seen *Friday The 13th* or *The Blair Witch Project*, but idyllic in every other sense).

8   I will never forget pulling back the curtains on the first morning. There were hummingbirds everywhere, whizzing backwards and forwards past the window like demented bees. Sometimes they paused in front of the sugar-water to feed, either perching or hovering with the immaculate precision of experienced helicopter pilots.

9   Apparently, it's possible to see as many as ten species at the ranch in just half an hour. But even when they stayed still for more than a few moments I had no idea which was which. As they moved around, their colours changed in relation to the angle of the sun. Bird identification is hard enough at the best of times, but this was ridiculous.

10   Take a male hummingbird, for example. When you look at it face-to-face its throat is a fiery scarlet red. But as it turns away the colour shifts – first to orange, then yellow, then blackish-brown and then green. Try identifying that in a hurry, before it turns

into a blur and helicopters away.

11   I think there were Anna's hummingbirds, black-chinned, broad billed, blue-throated, magnificent, red and violet-crowned that morning, but I'm not entirely sure. Later, I asked other bird-watchers about similar-looking hummers around "their" feeding station, but they weren't sure either. I left them bickering over the difference between the sapphire blue throat of a broad-bill and the cobalt blue throat of a blue-throat.

12   The biological advantage of changing colour is that the birds can control the way they look. If a male wants to impress a female he shows his best side, but if he wants to hide from a predator he merely turns away and almost disappears among the greenery.

13   According to Sheri Williamson, hummingbird expert and co-founder of the South-Eastern Arizona Bird Observatory, you can tell them apart by the sound of their wings. Broad-tailed hummingbirds, for example, have a metallic trill to their wingbeats, while male black-chinned hummingbirds make a dull, flat whine.

14   Sheri took me to see a hummingbird in the hand. There's a ringing station, or banding station as they call it in the States, at nearby Sierra Vista. It's open to the public and every weekend the observatory staff rig up a mist-net trap with a tasty-looking sugar-water feeder in the middle. Whenever a hummingbird dares an investigatory hover, a burly member of the observatory team rushes forward, waving his arms around, and ushers the unfortunate bird inside.

15   We caught lots of hummingbirds that day. One was a female black-chinned that squealed when she was caught. It was hard to tell whether this was out of fear or anger ("How could I, so fleet of wing, be caught by this enormous fool?"). We found her abdomen distended with an enormous egg, which Sheri guessed would be laid before nightfall.

16   For a brief moment, I actually held the delicate bundle of feathers in my hand, and was so nervous about squeezing too hard that she escaped. After hovering above us for a moment, she made a bee-line for the bushes.

17   Hovering hummingbirds draw crowds of naturalists from all over the world to South-East Arizona, but hovering does have one major drawback. Pound for pound, beating your wings 70 times per second uses more energy than any other activity in the animal kingdom. Living life in the fast lane means hummingbirds need a continuous supply of fuel.

18   A typical hummingbird eats around half its own weight in energy-rich nectar every day. To do that it has to keep others away from its favourite foodplants. I spent many hours watching them battle it out at feeding stations. Far from being all sweetness and light, they are little fighter pilots. If they were the size of ravens it wouldn't be safe to walk in the woods.

19   Before I left, there was one thing I had to do. Dutifully, I put on bright red lipstick, took a mouthful of sugar-water, sat back, puckered my lips . . . and waited. Within 30 seconds two hummingbirds came to investigate. Others soon followed.

20   I sat there for an eternity not daring to move. No hummingbird actually drank sugar-water from my mouth (who can blame them?), but several did hover so close I could feel their wingbeats against my cheeks.

21   Strangely, the encounter was every bit as impressive as rubbing shoulders with mountain gorillas in the wilds of Africa or performing slow-motion underwater ballets with dolphins in the Bahamas.

22   Even better, my biggest worry came to nothing – the red lipstick wiped off.

(*Adapted from an article by Mark Carwardine*)

[*END OF PASSAGE*]

[BLANK PAGE]

G

Total
Mark

0860/404

NATIONAL
QUALIFICATIONS
2004

WEDNESDAY, 5 MAY
1.00 PM – 1.50 PM

ENGLISH
STANDARD GRADE
General Level
Reading
Questions

Fill in these boxes and read what is printed below.

Full name of centre

Town

Forename(s)

Surname

Date of birth
Day Month Year

Scottish candidate number

Number of seat

**NB Before leaving the examination room you must give this booklet to the invigilator.
If you do not, you may lose all the marks for this paper.**

SCOTTISH
QUALIFICATIONS
AUTHORITY

©

Marks

QUESTIONS

Write your answers in the spaces provided.

Look at Paragraphs 1 and 2.

1. **Write down a word** from Paragraph 1 that suggests naturalists might be reluctant to kiss a hummingbird.

   _____

   2 ■ 0

2. Why are the hummingbirds attracted to someone wearing bright red lipstick?

   _____

   _____

   2 1 0

3. Why do you think the writer uses the word "theory" in Paragraph 2?

   _____

   2 ■ 0

Look at Paragraphs 3 and 4.

4. Where **exactly** did the writer first meet the hummingbirds?

   _____

   _____

   2 1 0

Look at Paragraphs 5 and 6.

5. Thousands of "hummers" (Paragraph 5)

   Why has the writer put the word "hummers" in inverted commas?

   _____

   _____

   2 ■ 0

PAGE
TOTAL

Marks

6. "Hanging from trees, bushes, fences and buildings they are full of a simple magic potion . . . flowers." (Paragraph 6)

   Identify and comment on the effect of **two features** of the structure of this sentence.

   (i) _____

   _____   2 1 0

   (ii) _____

   _____   2 1 0

7. **Write down an expression** from Paragraph 6 which tells you that the writer is surprised by the amount of sugar used.

   _____   2 ■ 0

Look at Paragraphs 7 and 8.

8. What do the expressions "whizzing" and "like demented bees" tell you about the movement of the hummingbirds?

   _____

   _____   2 1 0

9. **Write down an expression** which shows that the writer admires the flying skills of the hummingbird.

   _____   2 ■ 0

Look at Paragraphs 9 and 10.

10. **In your own words** write down **two** reasons why the writer found bird identification "ridiculous".   2 1 0

    (i) _____

    (ii) _____

PAGE
TOTAL

Marks

Look at Paragraphs 11 and 12.

11. What does the writer's use of the word "bickering" tell you about his attitude to the bird watchers?

_____   2 ■ 0

12. **In your own words** give **two** reasons why hummingbirds change their colour.   2 1 0

   (i) _____

   (ii) _____

Look at Paragraphs 13 to 15.

13. How does Sheri Williamson tell the difference between hummingbirds?

_____

_____   2 1 0

14. Comment on the writer's use of the expression "hummingbird in the hand".

_____

_____   2 1 0

15. "Whenever a hummingbird dares an investigatory hover, a burly member of the observatory team rushes forward, waving his arms around" (Paragraph 14)

   How does this description create effective contrasts?

   (i) _____   2 ■ 0

   (ii) _____   2 ■ 0

Look at Paragraph 16.

16. What does the expression "I actually held" tell you about how the writer felt when he held the hummingbird?

_____

_____   2 ■ 0

PAGE
TOTAL

Marks

Look at Paragraphs 17 and 18.

17. "Living life in the fast lane means hummingbirds need a continuous supply of fuel."
(Paragraph 17)

Explain the effectiveness of this image.

_____

_____

_____   2 | 1 | 0

18. **In your own words**, what **two** new impressions does the writer give of the hummingbird in Paragraph 18?

_____

_____   2 | 1 | 0

Look at Paragraphs 19 to 22.

19. "Dutifully, I put on bright red lipstick . . . puckered my lips . . . and waited."
(Paragraph 19)

Identify and comment on any **one feature** of structure **or** punctuation in this sentence.

_____

_____

_____   2 | 1 | 0

20. **Write down an expression** from Paragraph 20 which tells us the writer felt he waited for a long time.

_____   2 | ■ | 0

21. **In your own words** what does the writer's use of the word "Strangely" tell you about his reaction to the encounter with the hummingbirds?

_____

_____   2 | ■ | 0

[Turn over for Questions 22 and 23 on *Page six*

PAGE
TOTAL

Marks

Think about the passage as a whole.

22. From the passage **write down an example** of the writer's use of humour.

    Explain why it is effective.

    _____

    _____

    _____　2　1　0

23. Overall how do you think the writer feels about his experience with the humming-birds?

    Support your answer by referring to the passage.

    _____

    _____

    _____　2　1　0

[END OF QUESTION PAPER]

PAGE
TOTAL

[BLANK PAGE]

F

0860/401

NATIONAL	WEDNESDAY, 4 MAY	ENGLISH
QUALIFICATIONS	10.35 AM – 11.25 AM	STANDARD GRADE
2005		Foundation Level
		Reading
		Text

Read carefully the passage overleaf. It will help if you read it twice. When you have done so, answer the questions. Use the spaces provided in the Question/Answer booklet.

SCOTTISH
QUALIFICATIONS
AUTHORITY

1   When he first woke up, Pete Smeaton was sure he was still dreaming.

2   Then he opened his eyes and knew that it had really happened. He was lying in a sleeping bag on the floor of a room in his new home. A home he had never set eyes on before.

3   And Jenny was crying.

4   At least some things never changed.

5   Pete sat up stiffly and looked around. Whatever room he was in was furnished with nothing but packing cartons stacked one on top of the other. He couldn't tell if the room was large or small because all he could see were boxes, labelled in his mother's hasty scrawl:

Kitchen, My room, Hall, Pete, Jenny.

6   He remembered the hurried squeak of the marker pen on the boxes as the carrier waited to transport them up from London. That was just yesterday.

7   Even muffled by packing cartons, Jenny's cry was shrill and piercing. Pete groaned and flopped back on his sleeping bag. He closed his eyes and put his hands over his ears. The crying grew louder. Pete opened one eye, as Jenny was shoved into his arms.

8   "Take her, will you, so I can at least go to the toilet on my own. If I put her down she'll be sick. This new place is giving her the heebie-jeebies. She was up all night."

9   Pete's mother left him with the hot, open-mouthed bundle that was his baby sister. Three months old and more hassle than twenty Petes had ever been, according to Mrs Smeaton.

10   Pete stared into the tiny, furious face.

11   "Hel–lo noisy," he said slowly. Secretly, he loved the feeling of Jenny when he held her although he would never admit that out loud to anyone. No way!

12   Hearing Pete's voice, Jenny stopped crying instantly. Pete felt her body relax in his arms.

13   "Why d'you always stop crying for me, you little monkey?" Pete whispered on Jenny's downy head. "You should give Mum a break."

14   Fitting Jenny expertly in the crook of one arm, Pete levered himself up from the floor.

15   "C'mon let's see what this place is like, Jenny. Time to explore."

16   The floorboards felt rough and chilly under Pete's feet. Snuggling Jenny close he went out into the hallway.

17   "Must have slept in the lounge," Pete figured. He was downstairs and the only other room on this floor was a large square kitchen with a small scullery. Beyond lay a wild-looking garden.

18   "It's a jungle out there, Jenny," said Pete in an American accent. "Better wait till I'm armed before I investigate."

19   Upstairs, on the half landing of the house there was a bathroom and one huge empty bedroom. The morning sun streamed through its emptiness illuminating the specks of dust which danced in such numbers that the room appeared in soft focus.

20   Pete stood in the centre of this room and knew that he wanted it to be his. It was at least three times the size of his old bedroom in London.

21   Quickly, he planned where he would put his books and lean his guitar. His bed would fit perfectly in that corner over there, and if his desk fitted under the window he'd be able to look outside and daydream while he was supposed to be doing his homework.

22   There'd be enough room for all his friends to stay overnight if they brought their sleeping bags.

23   "We could have a midnight feast and make up all those songs that drive Mum mad and . . ."

24   Pete was whispering excitedly to Jenny. Then he remembered where he was now:

25   "What an idiot. What friends?" he said bitterly to Jenny. "Don't know anyone here, do I? Never even heard of Clydebank before in my life. Don't even know what bloomin' school I'll be going to."

26   Pete stared into Jenny's blue unblinking eyes.

27   "You're lucky. Bet we'll be back in London by the time you need any friends. How am I going to meet anyone here?"

28   Pete leaned his forehead despondently on the glass and stared down at the garden. It really did look like a jungle. An expanse of unruly grasses weaved before Pete, reaching down to a ramshackle brick outbuilding. Beyond that, the boundary of the garden was drawn by a row of mature trees and bushes.

29   "It's huge," thought Pete, who had never lived in a house with a garden before. He had to admit—grudgingly—that this garden looked big enough for a decent game of football. It was his birthday next week. Maybe he'd ask for goalposts instead of that portable CD player he had his eye on.

30   Pete gazed out the window and saw himself running out onto the grass heading a crowd of boys:

31   "Good pass, Pete."

32   "Here, over to me, Pete."

33   "Yeah, nice one, Pete."

34   "Pete, Pete."

35   "Pete? Where on earth have you gone?"

36   Mrs Smeaton's irritation interrupted his daydream.

37   "What you doing with her now? It's all dusty up here." She shuddered, "Ugh! And chilly."

38   Mrs Smeaton yanked Jenny from Pete's arms. She was asleep, a smug little smile playing over her lips.

39   "Now look what you've done," Mrs Smeaton's voice rose in frustration. "I wanted to feed her first."

40   Pete shrugged, "Sorry, Mum. She was awake two minutes ago. Honest." He was going to add, "Got the magic touch, haven't I?" but something about his mum's pinched face and tired, shaky voice made him stop. She looked as though she was going to start crying again. He really hated that. Never could get used to it, even though she cried all the time these days. Her tears made Pete feel panicky and scared.

41   Quickly he asked, "Mum, can I have this room if you and Dad don't want it?"

42   "Do what you like," snapped the answer. "Won't make any difference to me. I don't sleep these days with this one yammering all the time. Someone in this family might as well use one of the bedrooms to get some rest."

43   The bitterness in his mother's voice made Pete wince. He stood at the door of his new room watching her slump wearily downstairs with Jenny in her arms. There was a horrible tight feeling inside his chest.

44   By the time Mrs Smeaton had reached the bottom stair, Jenny was wailing.

45   "Oh, for goodness' sake," Pete heard his mother sigh, as she carried Jenny through to the kitchen, slamming the door behind her so hard that the whole house shook.

46   Then the wailing became louder. And louder still. It turned into sobbing. Huge, uncontrollable sobbing. Pete stood with his hand on the door knob and listened.

47   "Mum?"

48   Pete was more taken aback by the power of the crying than by the crying itself. Surely it wasn't Jenny? It was much too powerful. Whoever was crying was much closer than the kitchen downstairs. And it sounded like a child. Right next to Pete.

Adapted from *Think Me Back* by Catherine Forde

[END OF PASSAGE]

FOR OFFICIAL USE

F

Total Mark

0860/402

NATIONAL QUALIFICATIONS 2005

WEDNESDAY, 4 MAY 10.35 AM – 11.25 AM

ENGLISH STANDARD GRADE
Foundation Level
Reading
Questions

Fill in these boxes and read what is printed below.

Full name of centre

Town

Forename(s)

Surname

Date of birth

Day Month Year   Scottish candidate number   Number of seat

NB Before leaving the examination room you must give this booklet to the invigilator. If you do not, you may lose all the marks for this paper.

SCOTTISH QUALIFICATIONS AUTHORITY

QUESTIONS

Write your answers in the spaces provided.

Look at Paragraphs 1 to 4.

1. What was Pete's first thought when he woke up?

_____

2. What important event had just happened in Pete's life?

_____

3. "At least some things never changed."

What does this sentence suggest?

_____

_____

Look at Paragraphs 5 and 6.

4. "mother's hasty scrawl:"

(a) Give **two** reasons why the writer uses this expression to describe the writing on the boxes.

(i) _____

(ii) _____

(b) **Write down one word** from Paragraph 6 which continues this idea.

[   ]

Look at Paragraph 7.

5. **Write down two words** which describe Jenny's cry.

[   ]   [   ]

	Marks	
2	■	0
2	■	0
2	■	0
2	1	0
2	■	0
2	1	0

PAGE
TOTAL

Marks

6. How did Pete feel about Jenny's crying?

_____   2 ■ 0

Look at Paragraphs 8 to 10.

7. **Give two reasons** why Pete's mother asked him to hold the baby.   2 1 0

(i) _____

(ii) _____

8. **Write down an expression** which tells you that Pete had been an easier baby than Jenny.

_____   2 ■ 0

Look at Paragraphs 11 to 13.

9. Look at the final sentence of Paragraph 11.

How does the writer show Pete's strong feelings through

(i) sentence structure? _____

_____

(ii) punctuation? _____

_____   2 1 0

10. How did hearing Pete's voice affect Jenny?

_____   2 1 0

11. **Write down the expression** which shows that Pete felt sorry for his mum.

```
┌─────────────────────────────────────┐
│                                      │
│                                      │
└─────────────────────────────────────┘
```
2 ■ 0

[Turn over

PAGE
TOTAL

Marks

Look at Paragraphs 14 to 19.

12. **Write down one word** which shows that Pete was good at looking after his little sister.

    [   ]

    2 ■ 0

13. "Snuggling Jenny close" (Paragraph 16)

    Why did Pete do this?

    _____

    _____

    2 1 0

Look at Paragraphs 20 to 25.

14. Write down any **three** things which Pete liked about the room.

    2 1 0

    (i) _____

    (ii) _____

    (iii) _____

15. "We could have a midnight feast and make up all those songs that drive Mum mad and . . ." (Paragraph 23)

    Why did Pete not finish what he was saying?

    _____

    _____

    2 1 0

Look at Paragraphs 26 to 28.

16. **Write down the word** which shows that Pete thought there was no hope of having friends in his new home.

    [   ]

    2 ■ 0

PAGE
TOTAL

Marks

17. Write down three expressions which tell you that the garden had not been looked after.

| 2 | 1 | 0 |

(i) _____

(ii) _____

(iii) _____

Look at Paragraphs 29 to 34.

18. While daydreaming about the garden Pete imagined himself to be:

a football player ☐

a football referee ☐

a football fan ☐

| 2 | ■ | 0 |

Tick (✓) the correct box.

Look at Paragraphs 35 to 40.

19. "Mrs Smeaton's irritation interrupted his daydream." (Paragraph 36)

Write down two words from later **in this section of the passage** which develop the idea that Mrs Smeaton was angry.

| 2 | 1 | 0 |

20. What **three** things stopped Pete from continuing to answer his mother back?

| 2 | 1 | 0 |

(i) _____

(ii) _____

(iii) _____

Look at Paragraphs 41 to 48.

21. "Mum, can I have this room if you and Dad don't want it?" (Paragraph 41)

Why did Pete ask his mum this question at this time?

_____

| 2 | ■ | 0 |

[Turn over for Questions 22 to 24 on *Page six*

PAGE TOTAL

Marks

22. Write down three expressions which the writer uses to show that Pete's mother was still angry.

2	1	0

   (i) _____

   (ii) _____

   (iii) _____

23. "Surely it wasn't Jenny?" (Paragraph 48)

What **two** things made Pete think this?

2	1	0

   (i) _____

   (ii) _____

Think about the passage as a whole.

24. Tick (✓) **two words** which you think best describe Pete's character.

Give evidence from the passage to support your choices.

2	1	0

Caring   ☐

Imaginative   ☐

Moody   ☐

Sensitive   ☐

   (i) _____

       _____

   (ii) _____

       _____

[END OF QUESTION PAPER]

PAGE
TOTAL

[BLANK PAGE]

G

0860/403

NATIONAL
QUALIFICATIONS
2005

WEDNESDAY, 4 MAY
1.00 PM – 1.50 PM

ENGLISH
STANDARD GRADE
General Level
Reading
Text

Read carefully the passage overleaf. It will help if you read it twice. When you have done so, answer the questions. Use the spaces provided in the Question/Answer booklet.

SCOTTISH
QUALIFICATIONS
AUTHORITY

Dazzled by the Stars

Our love affair with fame may be bad for our health, according to new research. **John Harlow** reports on "celebrity worship syndrome".

1 Under her bed Katherine Hicks keeps six years of yellowing newspaper clippings about the former pop band Boyzone, and 70 videos of their performances. There might have been more if her attention had not moved on to Westlife, another pop sensation.

2 In one year she has spent £3,000 to watch Westlife perform 17 times, and is such a regular concert fan that she believes the band now recognise her as an acquaintance, if not a friend.

3 She has fixed her sights on a new star: David Sneddon, first winner of the television show Fame Academy. She cornered Sneddon at two television appearances, though it is early days in her "acquaintance" with him. Yet she felt forced to defend him indignantly against a TV presenter who, she thought, had not shown Sneddon sufficient respect.

4 Hicks is no deluded young teen: she is a 28-year-old electrical engineer. But she freely admits to an "addiction" to the latest musical sensations. "I have an obsessive nature. Anything I do is full-on, but it has never caused me problems," she said last week. "I don't do anything I cannot afford, and I don't ring in sick at work to get time off."

5 She is no stalker or obsessive; she is just "fascinated by the real personas of these people". Though she likens her behaviour to an "addiction rather than an illness", she sees nothing odd in it.

6 "Other people think I am ill or sad," she said, "but I am not missing out on anything."

7 Psychologists, who are taking an increasing interest in the effects of celebrity culture, might disagree. As Anglo-American research published last week reveals, our relationship with celebrities is more complicated than we realise. The strength of our interest in celebrities, say academics, may affect our mood.

8 Lynn McCutcheon, of DeVry University in Florida, John Maltby, of Leicester University, and two colleagues will publish a book next year exposing the psychological needs and drives behind celebrity worship.

9 But initial results of research they have conducted show that about a third of people suffer from what the researchers call "celebrity worship syndrome" and it affects their mental wellbeing.

10 It raises a troubling question: in the era of "industrialised fame", is hero worship bad for you?

11 Perhaps we should blame the start of it on Alexander the Great who, more than 2,000 years ago, exploited to the full the idea of the beautiful "god-king".

12 But if celebrity has been a cultural phenomenon for centuries, why should it have become a problem now? McCutcheon and Maltby believe the scale of it has made a huge jump in recent years. The average westerner is now exposed to hundreds of star images every day, through advertising, broadcasting, fashion, the internet and innumerable other forms.

13 Though sales of some celebrity magazines are slipping, figures show that new publications are thriving. In America, the thirst for star images is so strong that one photographer was recently paid £70,000 for a single picture.

14 David Beckham is now so famous that one paper set out on a humorous quest to find someone who did not know who he was: they finally tracked down an innocent in the Saharan city of Timbuktu.

15 The rapid growth of fan-based internet sites spreads gossip, the lifeblood of celebrity, at lightning speed. There are

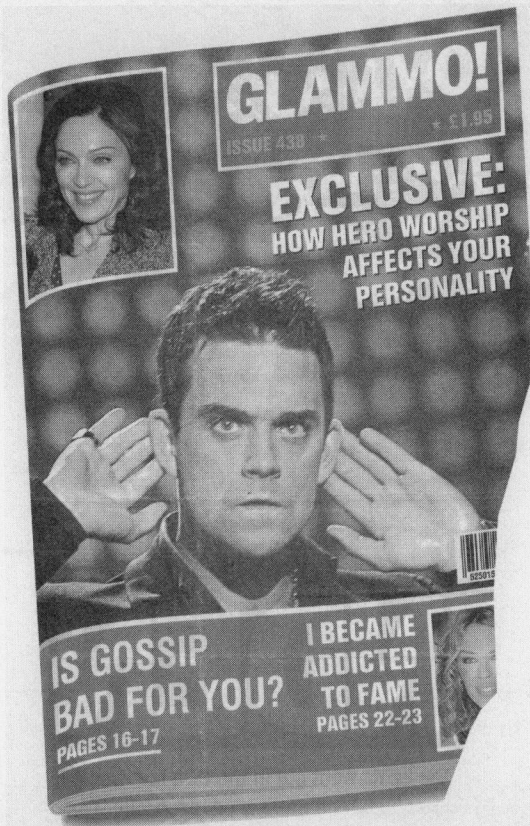

more than 100,000 sites dedicated to Madonna alone.

16   Such a speedy development has prompted the academics to create the celebrity attitude scale. Using a series of questions designed to gauge personality and the level of interest in celebrities, they surveyed 700 people.

17   Most were just casually interested in stars. But one in five people displayed a determined interest. They even rearrange their social lives, for example, to follow their chosen celebrity.

18   Some 10% of people displayed such "intense-personal" attitudes towards celebrities that they showed signs of addiction.

19   It can lead to extreme actions. On both sides of the Atlantic, some fans have resorted to plastic surgery to look more like their heroes. A Scottish actor had himself turned into a Pierce Brosnan lookalike and admits he now often walks and talks like 007.

20   Dr Nicholas Chugay, a Beverly Hills surgeon, has turned various Californians into Elvis Presley or Cher. "I have had to turn some people away because I do not feel it would be good for them to let such worship take over their lives," said Chugay.

21   BUT it may not be all that bad. Indeed, other academics argue that the likes of Beckham and Madonna are even good for you. They say that celebrity culture is based on sound reasons: by watching and imitating our so-called betters, whether it be in clothes or habits, we learn to flourish in human society.

22   Francisco Gil-White, of Pennsylvania University, argues we need celebrities to show us the road to success. He says they provide the educational and entertaining fables once sought in fairy tales.

23   "It makes sense to copy winners, because whoever is getting more of what everybody wants, and in this society this includes media attention, is probably using successful methods to get it."

24   But though some role models, such as Gareth Gates, the singer, and Tiger Woods, the golfer, can maintain they are blazing a trail for others to follow, can less worthy idols cause damage? Nancy Salzburg, who is researching charisma at San Diego University, said bad idols can cause trouble for their followers.

25   Choose well and there are benefits in celebrity, says Maltby. "It may help people to develop a relationship with and understand the world. If you admire someone like David Beckham, for example, and follow his dietary regime and the way he plays football, there can be a positive outcome in doing that."

26   Mark Griffiths, a professor of psychology at Nottingham Trent University, agrees.

27   "It was quite clear that for fans their idols formed a healthy part of their life," he said. "It was a way of raising their self-esteem.

28   What has happened is that people are not so religious and they don't look up to political and religious leaders any more. They have been replaced by the David Beckhams and the pop stars and film stars. That's who you see on the walls of teenagers' rooms because these are the people they look up to and admire."

Adapted from an article by
John Harlow

[END OF PASSAGE]

[BLANK PAGE]

FOR OFFICIAL USE

G

Total Mark

0860/404

NATIONAL QUALIFICATIONS 2005

WEDNESDAY, 4 MAY
1.00 PM – 1.50 PM

ENGLISH
STANDARD GRADE
General Level
Reading
Questions

Fill in these boxes and read what is printed below.

Full name of centre

Town

Forename(s)

Surname

Date of birth
Day Month Year

Scottish candidate number

Number of seat

NB Before leaving the examination room you must give this booklet to the invigilator.
If you do not, you may lose all the marks for this paper.

SCOTTISH
QUALIFICATIONS
AUTHORITY

Marks

QUESTIONS

Write your answers in the spaces provided.

Look at Paragraphs 1 and 2.

1. What evidence is there to suggest that Katherine Hicks was a keen fan of Boyzone?

   _____

   _____ 2 1 0

2. **Write down three key facts** which clearly show that Katherine Hicks is now a keen Westlife fan. 2 1 0

   (i) _____

   (ii) _____

   (iii) _____

Look at Paragraph 3.

3. Why do you think the writer uses the expression "fixed her sights"?

   _____

   _____ 2 ■ 0

4. "early days in her "acquaintance" with him"

   Why has the writer put the word "acquaintance" in inverted commas?

   _____

   _____ 2 ■ 0

5. What do the words "forced" and "indignantly" in Paragraph 3 tell you about Katherine's reactions to the TV presenter's treatment of David Sneddon?

   _____ 2 1 0

PAGE
TOTAL

Marks

Look at Paragraphs 4 to 6.

6. "Hicks is no deluded young teen: she is a 28-year-old electrical engineer." (Paragraph 4)

   What does this statement tell you about the writer's attitude towards Katherine's behaviour?

   _____ 2 ■ 0

7. (a) Which of the following best describes Katherine's attitude towards her "addiction"?

   Tick (✓) the appropriate box.

   Concerned   ☐

   Guilty   ☐

   Relaxed   ☐   2 ■ 0

   (b) **Quote an expression** to support your answer.

   _____ 2 ■ 0

Look at Paragraphs 7 to 10.

8. **Give three reasons** why psychologists are showing an increasing interest in "celebrity culture".   2 1 0

   (i) _____

   (ii) _____

   (iii) _____

9. Explain why the writer ends Paragraph 10 with a question.

   _____ 2 ■ 0

Marks

Look at Paragraphs 11 to 14.

10. Who does the writer suggest is to blame for the start of hero worship?

_____

2 ■ 0

11. Quote an expression which shows that celebrity worship is nothing new.

_____

2 ■ 0

12. In your own words explain why the scale of hero worship has made a huge jump in recent years.

_____

_____

_____

2 1 0

13. What does the word "thirst" suggest about the American attitude towards celebrity gossip?

_____

_____

2 ■ 0

14. Why do you think the writer includes the information about the quest in Paragraph 14?

_____

_____

2 1 0

Look at Paragraphs 15 to 18.

15. What has helped to spread celebrity gossip at great speed?

_____

2 ■ 0

PAGE
TOTAL

Marks

16. **In your own words** what is the "celebrity attitude scale" designed to reveal?

_____

_____   2 | 1 | 0

Look at Paragraphs 19 and 20.

17. In what **two** ways does the writer show the extent of celebrity "addiction"?   2 | 1 | 0

(i) _____

(ii) _____

Look at Paragraphs 21 to 24.

18. Why does the writer put the word "BUT" in capital letters at the beginning of Paragraph 21?

_____

_____   2 | 1 | 0

19. In the opinion of Francisco Gil-White, what important influence have celebrities replaced?

_____   2 | ■ | 0

20. What does the writer's use of the expression "blazing a trail" (Paragraph 24) tell you about Gareth Gates and Tiger Woods?

_____

_____   2 | ■ | 0

[Turn over for Questions 21, 22 and 23 on *Page six*

PAGE TOTAL

Marks

Look at Paragraphs 25 to 28.

21. **In your own words** what, according to Maltby, could be the positive outcomes of admiring David Beckham?

_____

_____   2 1 0

22. According to Mark Griffiths:

    (*a*) how can idols form a healthy part of people's lives?

    Answer in your own words.

    _____

    _____   2 ■ 0

    (*b*) why have pop stars and film stars replaced political and religious leaders?
    Tick (✓) the appropriate box.

    They are good looking.   ☐

    They are easily recognised.   ☐

    They are respected and highly regarded. ☐   2 ■ 0

Think about the passage as a whole.

23. "DAZZLED BY THE STARS"

    Explain why, in your opinion, this is an **appropriate** title.

    _____

    _____

    _____   2 1 0

[END OF QUESTION PAPER]

PAGE
TOTAL

[BLANK PAGE]

F

0860/401

| NATIONAL QUALIFICATIONS | WEDNESDAY, 3 MAY | ENGLISH |
| 2006 | 10.35 AM – 11.25 AM | STANDARD GRADE |

NATIONAL
QUALIFICATIONS
2006

WEDNESDAY, 3 MAY
10.35 AM – 11.25 AM

ENGLISH
STANDARD GRADE
Foundation Level
Reading
Text

Read carefully the passage overleaf. It will help if you read it twice. When you have done so, answer the questions. Use the spaces provided in the Question/Answer booklet.

Ain't no mountain high enough

Scott Cory is only 14 but he's already scaled some of the highest, most dangerous rock-faces in the world. **Deborah Netburn** watches "Spider-Boy" in action in California.

1　As she stands in the valley of Yosemite National Park, northern California, Jennifer Cory stares intently through a high-powered telescope trained at a great wall of forbidding grey granite which juts high above the alpine meadow. Though she may look like a devoted bird-watcher, the dark-haired 38-year-old is actually keeping a close eye on her 14-year-old son, the American rock-climbing sensation Scott Cory, who is scaling the 2,900 ft wall. High above his mother, the sandy-haired boy keeps his body pressed close against the wall as he calmly scans the rock for the next tiny nick to use as a hand or foot hold. He makes his way quickly and methodically up the great wall. When at last he comes to a pitch (a small ledge to use as a resting place) he stops and calmly looks down at the forest landscape a full skyscraper's length below him. "He looks just as comfortable as if he was standing in his own front yard," says his mother.

2　This trip to Yosemite, two hours from the Corys' home just north of San Francisco, is part of Scott's training for two rock-climbing feats he has planned for the summer. This week he will climb El Capitan and Half Dome. Then, in August, Scott and his fellow rock-climber Steve Schneider, 43, will fly to Lima, Peru, where they plan to be the first Americans to climb "Welcome to the Slabs of Koricancha", a 2,000 ft near-vertical route up La Esfinge mountain. What makes this climb particularly difficult, besides the few hand and foot holds, is the high altitude. The base of the route is 14,000 ft. But Scott seems unconcerned. "It looks like a lot of fun," he tells me.

3　Although Scott hasn't entered high school yet, he has all the trappings of a sports superstar: a sponsorship clothing deal that he picked up at the age of seven; his own sports agent (who also represents Anna Kournikova); and a lot of media coverage (he's appeared on TV and in *Sports Illustrated* in America). Thanks to his good looks he is also starting to build a female fanbase: in one web chatroom a teenage girl listed him as one of her three favourite stars along with Orlando Bloom and Johnny Depp.

4　Scott, who started climbing on a family holiday when he was 7, set his first record when he was 11 by becoming the youngest person to climb "The Nose" of El Capitan, one of the world's most famous and difficult climbing routes. One month later he became the youngest person to do the climb in one day. Fellow rock-climbers say they admire the dedication that has kept this 14-year-old in the gym for four days a week, five hours a day for the past seven years.

5　"I think what sets Scotty apart from a lot of kids," says Beth Rodden, 23, a climber who has known Scott since he was seven, "is that he is up for any challenge, and that is really the key to his success."

6　Scott's explanation of what keeps him in the gym instead of in front of a PlayStation is simple and short. "I love it, and it's fun for me."

7　Indeed, away from the rock-face, in a café down the street from the University of California at Berkeley, Scott looks and acts entirely his age.

8　At the café, Scott is joined by his "mom" Jennifer, and his dad, Jim.

9　Scott orders a pizza, but when it comes he sends it back because the chef has forgotten to hold the anchovies. To tide him over the waitress brings a small leek and onion tart.

10　Scott eyes the tart suspiciously.

11　"Try it," says his mother.

Scott Cory climbing in Red Rocks, Nevada

12   "You try it, Dad," says Scott, moving the plate closer to his father.

13   An hour later he is back in his element at the Touchstone rock-climbing gym at Mission Cliffs in San Francisco. Gyms like these are becoming increasingly popular in the United States; in the early 1990s there were around five, today there are over 500. Scott bounds through the glass doors, nods hello to a man working at the front desk, and steps into a harness. He clips on a little satchel containing powdery chalk to keep his hands dry, and pulls on a tiny pair of rock-climbing shoes.

14   "Scott usually wears a size nine but those shoes are six and a half," observes his father. "He crams his toes in there so he can feel every little thing when he is climbing the wall."

15   Within ten minutes Scott is moving swiftly up the artificial rock-face. The press has nicknamed him "Spider-Boy" because of his technique, though he says nobody calls him that in real life. But the nickname is good—the way he holds his body parallel to the wall, the way he makes full use of the span of his arms and legs, the trail of rope he leaves behind him as he climbs. In the gym, where he is able to study the routes from the ground, his climbing is more graceful than it is on the mountain.

16   Scott is still unsure what sort of future he will have in rock-climbing.

17   "I think he would love to see himself climbing for a living, but it just isn't a big enough sport," says his mother. "The professional climbers he knows just get by on a measly existence, but he hasn't even entered high school yet, so we have to see what happens. He could decide tomorrow that he doesn't like it anymore. Although I don't think anyone imagines that will happen."

18   Back on the wall Scott works on the final section of the hardest route. Grasping the small rubber holds he swiftly moves upwards. Below, his friends in the gym cheer for him, but just as he reaches the top his hand slips and he is left dangling in the air.

19   Scott has been here three hours already, and he has tried this particular route at least five times. His parents are ready to leave but Scott won't hear of it. He isn't going anywhere until he gets it right.

Adapted from the
Sunday Telegraph Magazine

[END OF PASSAGE]

[BLANK PAGE]

FOR OFFICIAL USE

F

Total Mark

0860/402

NATIONAL QUALIFICATIONS 2006

WEDNESDAY, 3 MAY 10.35 AM – 11.25 AM

ENGLISH STANDARD GRADE Foundation Level Reading Questions

Fill in these boxes and read what is printed below.

Full name of centre

Town

Forename(s)

Surname

Date of birth

Day Month Year   Scottish candidate number   Number of seat

NB Before leaving the examination room you must give this booklet to the invigilator. If you do not, you may lose all the marks for this paper.

SCOTTISH QUALIFICATIONS AUTHORITY

Marks

QUESTIONS

Write your answers in the spaces provided.

Look at Paragraph 1.

1. Where **exactly** in northern California is Jennifer Cory as she watches her son climb?

_____

2 1 0

2. Write down the expression which suggests that Jennifer is concentrating very hard on what she is doing.

_____

2 ■ 0

3. "Though she may look like a devoted bird-watcher . . ."

Give a reason why Jennifer could be mistaken for a bird-watcher.

_____

2 ■ 0

4. ". . . a great wall of forbidding grey granite . . ."

What impression do we get of the mountain from this description?

_____

2 1 0

5. **Write down three separate words** the writer uses in Paragraph 1 to suggest Scott Cory is a good climber.

2 1 0

6. ". . . **a full skyscraper's length below him**"

Explain fully why the writer uses this expression here.

_____

_____

2 1 0

PAGE
TOTAL

Marks

Look at Paragraph 2.

7. "'It looks like a lot of fun,' he tells me."

    Give **two** reasons why the reader might find Scott's statement surprising.

    (i) _____ | 2 | ■ | 0

    (ii) _____ | 2 | ■ | 0

Look at Paragraph 3.

8. (*a*)   Give **three** pieces of evidence that show Scott ". . . has all the trappings of a sports superstar".

    _____

    _____ | 2 | 1 | 0

    (*b*)   Why are the words *Sports Illustrated* in italics?

    _____ | 2 | ■ | 0

Look at Paragraph 4.

9. What were the first **two** climbing records which Scott set?

    (i) _____ | 2 | 1 | 0

    (ii) _____ | 2 | 1 | 0

10. Write down **one word** which **sums up** Scott's attitude to training.

    | 2 | ■ | 0

    [Turn over

PAGE TOTAL

Marks

Look at Paragraphs 7 to 12.

11. Why does the writer put inverted commas around "mom"?

_____

2 ■ 0

12. In the café, how does Scott behave like a typical teenager?

_____

_____

2 1 0

Look at Paragraphs 13 and 14.

13. What evidence does the writer give to show that rock climbing gyms ". . . are becoming increasingly popular" (Paragraph 13)?

_____

2 1 0

14. Write down an expression from Paragraph 13 which suggests Scott is eager to begin training.

_____

2 ■ 0

15. (*a*) Why does Scott have to "cram" his toes into his rock-climbing shoes?

_____

2 ■ 0

(*b*) What does he gain from doing this?

_____

2 ■ 0

PAGE
TOTAL

Marks

Look at Paragraph 15.

16. (*a*) "The press has nicknamed him Spider-Boy . . ."

Tick (✓) the **three best** reasons why, **according to the passage**, this is a good nickname.

2 | 1 | 0

His rope looks like a spider's thread. ☐

He is very young. ☐

He looks like a character from a comic. ☐

He uses his arms and legs at full stretch. ☐

He holds his body at the same angle as the wall. ☐

He is climbing indoors. ☐

(*b*) Which expression, **used later in the passage**, reminds the reader of this comparison with a spider?

_____

2 | ■ | 0

Look at Paragraphs 16 and 17.

17. **Write down an expression** which suggests that some professional climbers do not make much money from the sport.

_____

2 | ■ | 0

Look at Paragraphs 18 and 19.

18. What **two** pieces of evidence show that Scott does not like to give up on a climb?

_____

_____

2 | 1 | 0

[Turn over for Question 19 on *Page six*

☐

PAGE
TOTAL

Think about the passage as a whole.

Marks

19. (a) What impression do you, as a reader, get of Scott Cory?

_____ 2 ■ 0

(b) Give **two** pieces of evidence from the passage to support your answer.

_____

_____ 2 1 0

[*END OF QUESTION PAPER*]

PAGE
TOTAL

[BLANK PAGE]

G

0860/403

NATIONAL
QUALIFICATIONS
2006

WEDNESDAY, 3 MAY
1.00 PM – 1.50 PM

ENGLISH
STANDARD GRADE
General Level
Reading
Text

Read carefully the passage overleaf. It will help if you read it twice. When you have done so, answer the questions. Use the spaces provided in the Question/Answer booklet.

SCOTTISH
QUALIFICATIONS
AUTHORITY

In this extract from a novel set in a secondary school, the narrator, John, is sitting in his Maths class. Gloria (nicknamed Glory Hallelujah) is another pupil in the same class.

1   I am sitting in school, in Maths, with a piece of paper in my hand. No, it is not my algebra homework. It is not a quiz that I have finished and am waiting to hand in to Mrs Moonface. The piece of paper in my hand has nothing at all to do with Mathematics. Nor does it have to do with any school subject. Nor is it really a piece of paper at all.

2   It is really my fate, masquerading as paper.

3   I am sitting next to Glory Hallelujah and I am waiting for a break in the action. Mrs Moonface is at the front of the room, going on about integers. I am not hearing a single thing that she is saying. She could stop lecturing about integers and start doing a cancan kick or singing a rap song and I would not notice.

4   She could call on me and ask me any question on earth, and I would not be able to answer.

5   But luckily, she does not call on me. She has a piece of chalk in her right hand. She is waving it around like a dagger as she spews algebra gibberish at a hundred miles a minute.

6   I hear nothing. Algebra does not have the power to penetrate my feverish isolation.

7   You see, I am preparing to ask Glory Hallelujah out on a date.

8   I am on an island, even though I am sitting at my desk surrounded by my classmates.

9   I am on Torture Island.

10   There are no trees on Torture Island—no huts, no hills, no beaches. There is only doubt.

11   Gloria will laugh at me. That thought is my lonely and tormenting company here on Torture Island. The exact timing and nature of her laughter are open to endless speculation.

12   She may not take me seriously. Her response may be "Oh, John, do you exist? Are you here on earth with me? I wasn't aware we were sharing the same universe."

13   Or she may be even more sarcastic. "John, I would love to go on a date with you, but I'm afraid I have to change my cat's litter box that night ."

14   So, as you can see, Torture Island is not exactly a beach resort. I am not having much fun here. I am ready to seize my moment and leave Torture Island forever.

15   In registration, I ripped a piece of paper from my yellow notepad. My black ball-point pen shook slightly in my trembling right hand as I wrote out the fateful question: "Gloria, will you go out with me this Friday?" Beneath that monumental question, I drew two boxes. One box was conspicuously large. I labelled it the YES box. The second box was tiny. I labelled it the NO box.

16   And that is the yellow piece of paper I have folded up into a square and am holding in my damp hand as I wait here on Torture Island for Mrs Moonface to turn towards the blackboard and give me the opportunity I need.

17   I cannot approach Glory Hallelujah after class because she is always surrounded by her friends. I cannot wait and pass the note to her later in the week because she may make plans to go out with one of her girlfriends. No, it is very evident to me that today is the day, and that I must pass the note before this period ends or forever live a coward.

18   There are only ten minutes left in Maths and Mrs Moonface seems to have no intention of recording her algebraic observations for posterity. Perhaps the piece of yellow chalk in her hand is just a prop. It is possible that the previous night she hurt her wrist in an arm-wrestling competition and can no longer write. It is also possible that she has forgotten all about her pupils and believes that she is playing a part in a Hollywood movie.

19   There are only seven minutes left in Maths. I attempt to turn Mrs Moonface towards the blackboard by telekinesis. The atoms of her body prove remarkably resistant to my telepathic powers.

20   There are six minutes left. Now there are five.

21   Mrs Moonface, for Pete's sake, write something on the blackboard! That is what Mathematics teachers do! Write down axioms, simplify equations, draw rectangles, measure angles, even, if you must, sketch the sneering razor-toothed face of Algebra itself. WRITE ANYTHING!

22   Suddenly Mrs Moonface stops lecturing.

23   Her right hand, holding the chalk, rises.

24   Then her hips begin to pivot.

25   This all unfolds in very slow motion. The sheer importance of the moment slows the action way, way down.

26   The pivoting of Mrs Moonface's hips causes a corresponding rotation in the plane of her shoulders and upper torso.

27   Her neck follows her shoulders, as day follows night.

28   Eventually, the lunar surface of her face is pulled towards the blackboard.

29   She begins to write. I have no idea what she is writing. It could be hieroglyphics and I would not notice. It could be a map to Blackbeard's treasure and I would not care.

30   I am now primed. My heart is thumping against my ribs, one by one, like a hammer pounding out a musical scale on a metal keyboard. Bing. Bang. Bong. Bam. I am breathing so quickly that I cannot breathe, if that makes any sense.

31   I am aware of every single one of my classmates in Maths.

32   Everyone in Maths is now preoccupied. There are only four minutes left in the period. Mrs Moonface is filling up blackboard space at an unprecedented speed, no doubt trying to scrape every last kernel of mathematical knowledge from the corncob of her brain before the bell. My classmates are racing to keep up with her. All around me pens are moving across notebooks at such a rate that ink can barely leak out and affix itself to paper.

33   My moment is at hand! The great clapper in the bell of fate clangs for me! *Ka-wang! Ka-wang!*

34   My right hand rises and begins to move sideways, very slowly, like a submarine, travelling at sub-desk depth to avoid teacher radar.

35   My right index finger makes contact with the sacred warm left wrist of Glory Hallelujah!

36   She looks down to see who is touching her at sub-desk depth. Spots my hand, with its precious yellow note.

37   Gloria understands instantly.

38   The exchange of the covert note is completed in a nanoinstant. Mrs Moonface and the rest of our Maths class have no idea that anything momentous has taken place.

39   I reverse the speed and direction of my right hand, and it returns safely to port.

40   Gloria has transferred my note to her lap and has moved her right elbow to block anyone on that side of her from seeing. The desk itself provides added shielding.

41   In the clever safe haven that she has created, she unfolds my note. Reads it.

42   She does not need to speak. She does not need to check the YES or NO boxes on my note. If she merely blinks, I will understand. If she wrinkles her nose, the import of her nose wrinkle will not be lost on me. In fact, so total is my concentration in that moment of grand suspense I am absolutely positive that there is nothing that Glory Hallelujah can do, no reaction that she can give off, that I will not immediately and fully understand.

43   I would stake my life on it.

44   But what she does do is this. She folds my note back up. Without looking at me—without even an eye blink or a nose wrinkle—she raises it to her lips. For one wild instant I think that she is going to kiss it.

45   Her pearly teeth part.

46   She eats my note.

Adapted from the novel *"You Dont Know Me"* By David Klass

[END OF PASSAGE]

G

Total Mark

0860/404

NATIONAL
QUALIFICATIONS
2006

WEDNESDAY, 3 MAY
1.00 PM – 1.50 PM

ENGLISH
STANDARD GRADE
General Level
Reading
Questions

Fill in these boxes and read what is printed below.

Full name of centre

Town

Forename(s)

Surname

Date of birth
Day Month Year

Scottish candidate number

Number of seat

NB Before leaving the examination room you must give this booklet to the invigilator. If you do not, you may lose all the marks for this paper.

SCOTTISH
QUALIFICATIONS
AUTHORITY

Marks

QUESTIONS

Write your answers in the spaces provided.

Look at Paragraphs 1 to 4.

1. (*a*)   Who is Mrs Moonface?

_____   2 ■ 0

   (*b*)   Why do you think John gives her the nickname "Mrs Moonface"?

_____

_____   2 1 0

2. "It is really my fate, masquerading as paper."

Why does the writer place this sentence in a paragraph of its own?

_____

_____   2 1 0

3. "Mrs Moonface is at the front of the room, going on about integers."

What does the expression "going on" suggest about John's attitude to what Mrs Moonface is saying?

_____   2 ■ 0

Look at Paragraphs 5 to 10.

4. How does the writer make Mrs Moonface's behaviour seem threatening?

_____

_____   2 1 0

PAGE
TOTAL

Marks

5. ". . . spews algebra gibberish at a hundred miles a minute. . ." (Paragraph 5)

Explain in your own words what the writer's word choice in this expression suggests about what John thinks of:

 (i) **what** she is saying;

_____

_____ 2 ■ 0

 (ii) **how** she says it.

_____

_____ 2 ■ 0

6. ". . . I am preparing to ask Glory Hallelujah out on a date." (Paragraph 7)

Why do you think the writer waits until this point to reveal what John is planning to do?

_____

_____ 2 1 0

7. "I am on Torture Island." (Paragraph 9)

 (*a*) **Explain fully in your own words** what the narrator means by this.

_____

_____ 2 1 0

 (*b*) Write down an expression from later in the passage which contains a similar idea.

 ```
 _____
 |                                       |
 |                                       |
 |_____|
 ```
 2 ■ 0

[Turn over

PAGE
TOTAL

Marks

8. Explain how the writer emphasises the bleakness of "Torture Island".

_____

_____   2 1 0

Look at Paragraphs 11 to 14.

9. (*a*) **Write down an example** of the writer's use of humour in these paragraphs.

_____

_____   2 ■ 0

(*b*) Explain why your chosen example is funny.

_____

_____   2 1 0

Look at Paragraphs 15 to 17.

10. **Write down three** pieces of evidence that suggest the narrator's nervousness at this point in the story.

_____

_____

_____   2 1 0

11. Quote **two** separate words used by the writer to suggest the importance of what John is asking Gloria.

[   ]   [   ]   2 1 0

12. "One box was conspicuously large . . . The second box was tiny." (Paragraph 15)

Why do you think John makes the boxes different sizes?

_____

_____   2 1 0

PAGE
TOTAL

Marks

13. **In your own words**, give a reason why John must make his approach to Gloria during Maths.

_____

_____   2 | 1 | 0

Look at Paragraphs 18 to 21.

14. How does the writer suggest the mood of increasing tension at this point in the passage?

_____

_____   2 | ■ | 0

15. "WRITE ANYTHING!" (Paragraph 21)

Why are these words written in capital letters?

_____

_____   2 | ■ | 0

Look at Paragraphs 22 to 33

16. (a) Identify any **one** technique used by the writer in this section to suggest John's growing excitement.

_____   2 | ■ | 0

(b) Explain **how** it does so.

_____

_____   2 | 1 | 0

[Turn over for Questions 17 to 20 on *Page six*

PAGE
TOTAL

Marks

Look at Paragraphs 34 to 46.

17. Give **three** reasons why Mrs Moonface is unaware of the note being passed.

_____

_____

_____

2 | 1 | 0

18. Why does John feel the "YES" or "NO" boxes on his note are now irrelevant?

_____

_____

2 | 1 | 0

19. How does the final paragraph provide an effective end to the passage?

_____

_____

2 | 1 | 0

Now look at the passage as a whole.

20. How realistic do you find the writer's description of this classroom incident? Give reasons for your opinion.

_____

_____

_____

2 | 1 | 0

[END OF QUESTION PAPER]

PAGE
TOTAL

[BLANK PAGE]

F

0860/401

NATIONAL
QUALIFICATIONS
2007

TUESDAY, 1 MAY
10.35 AM – 11.25 AM

ENGLISH
STANDARD GRADE
Foundation Level
Reading
Text

Read carefully the passage overleaf. It will help if you read it twice. When you have done so, answer the questions. Use the spaces provided in the Question/Answer booklet.

SCOTTISH
QUALIFICATIONS
AUTHORITY

Why dumped dog is such a lucky hound

No one wanted greyhound Pal after he was abandoned for not being fast enough on the track—until an animal trainer was asked to find a dog to star in a film. DAVID WIGG tells how the renamed Celt so nearly lost out again—before finding a new home and some much-needed love.

1 As Celt the greyhound comes bounding over to me on green fields overlooking the picturesque fields of Kent, he obviously knows he is a dog in a million. Once abandoned, he is now the star of a heartwarming film.

2 Celt, with his golden fawn markings, is one of many unwanted greyhounds in Britain that are dumped if they don't come up to racing standards.

3 He had ended up being abandoned at a greyhound rescue centre. As the weeks went by, no one came to adopt Celt as a family pet but then something even more exciting happened to him.

4 Animal handler Sue Potter had been asked to find an appealing greyhound to star in the film entitled "The Mighty Celt", a touching story about a boy and his love and devotion for a dog he desperately wants to own.

5 Sue had the almost impossible task of choosing one greyhound from more than 100 at the kennels.

6 But when she saw Celt, or Pal, as he was then known, Sue immediately knew he was the one she could train for the film. So what was so special about Celt?

7 "His colouring was perfect, he had to be fawn with some white markings," says Sue. "He also had to be obedient and compatible with people and other animals.

8 "I tested his reaction to sound and that was fine. There couldn't be anything wrong with him—he had to be an entire dog."

9 Sue trained Celt for two weeks at her home in the north of England, in preparation for his starring role. Celt then spent eight weeks filming in Northern Ireland with the cast and crew.

10 From all accounts, Celt excelled himself on set and everyone fell in love with him, but after the filming there was one big question remaining—what was to become of Celt? After all the attention he had received, it didn't seem right that he should go back to being alone and unwanted once again at the kennels, but Sue felt she couldn't keep him as she already owned five dogs.

11 Urgent inquiries were made among the crew and cast but it seemed no one was able to take him on from the film set where he had been thoroughly pampered.

12 On hearing of the young dog's plight, Kent landowner and farmer Philip Daubeny came to the rescue. Philip is chairman of the London-based charity Dogs Trust, which cares for more than 12,500 strays each year.

13 He had recently lost his own pet greyhound Tocki, another rescued dog. To everyone's relief he agreed to adopt Celt and take him to his lovely country home surrounded by 500 acres of open

hills and farmland near Maidstone. Here Celt now enjoys long walks and romps with Philip's other pets—corgis Dusty and Yehudi and five cats.

14   With Celt looking a picture of contentment, fully spread out in an armchair, Philip recalls: "The first I heard of him was through a vet in Northern Ireland called Rose McIlrath.

15   "One of her friends, Claire Millar, was working as a teacher with the children on the film. When it turned out that no real provision had been made for what was going to happen to Celt, Claire asked Rose if she had any ideas.

16   "Rose immediately thought of me because I had recently lost Tocki, who had been with me for seven years." Philip felt there was one important question that had to be asked before he agreed to take on Celt.

17   How did the greyhound get on with cats? "I was concerned because, on the whole, greyhounds are well known for chasing small furry animals, either cats or small dogs, often mistaking them for the hare on the track. I didn't want some terrible tragedy to happen with my five cats.

18   "I was assured that, after coming back to this country, Celt had been living with cats in a temporary home and I was assured of his character and that he would make a wonderful pet."

19   It was then arranged for Celt to be shipped over to the Dogs Trust Kenilworth Rehoming Centre, in Warwickshire. There he was thoroughly checked over.

20   Celt was driven down in an animal ambulance from Warwickshire to his new home in Kent in July last year.

21   "He was slightly anxious but he quickly settled down. We let him out in the field to meet the other dogs. He got on immediately with them and was keener to play with them than they were with him. He fitted in very easily and quickly, and made himself at home by sitting on every chair he could.

22   "He also wanted to jump on the beds as well, but there isn't much room to sleep if you have a greyhound on board. People think greyhounds need a lot of exercise but, actually, there's nothing they like more than curling up in an armchair and watching television."

23   I couldn't help wondering if, having been pampered on set, Celt acted like a film star. The response was laughter as Philip recalls: "He was very active and bursting with energy.

24   "At first, he rushed around as if he were on a greyhound track but, otherwise, he was among the more likeable and less affected film stars.

25   "Most affectionate, very beautiful and a genuine, kind, loving dog, that is marvellous with children."

26   Dog trainer Sue Potter adds: "I didn't want to take Celt back to the kennels because he had had a life of luxury on the film. I asked around if anyone would like to adopt him. The young boy in the film, Tyrone, fancied having him, but his father was moving house so he said no.

27   "I wanted him to go to a nice home—and he couldn't have gone to a better one. He was very lucky because he really has fallen on his feet."

Adapted from an article by David Wigg

[*END OF PASSAGE*]

[BLANK PAGE]

FOR OFFICIAL USE

F

Total Mark

0860/402

NATIONAL QUALIFICATIONS 2007

TUESDAY, 1 MAY 10.35 AM – 11.25 AM

ENGLISH STANDARD GRADE Foundation Level Reading Questions

Fill in these boxes and read what is printed below.

Full name of centre

Town

Forename(s)

Surname

Date of birth
Day Month Year

Scottish candidate number

Number of seat

NB Before leaving the examination room you must give this booklet to the invigilator. If you do not, you may lose all the marks for this paper.

SCOTTISH QUALIFICATIONS AUTHORITY

SA 0860/402 6/38070

QUESTIONS

Write your answers in the spaces provided.

Look at the Introduction and Paragraphs 1 to 3.

1. (a) Write down **one** word from Paragraph 1 which suggests that Celt the greyhound is a fit and healthy dog.

2 ■ 0

   (b) Write down an expression from Paragraph 1 which suggests that this might not always have been the case.

2 ■ 0

2. "... don't come up to racing standards." (Paragraph 2)

   Write down an expression from the introduction to the passage which contains a similar idea.

   _____

2 ■ 0

Look at Paragraphs 4 and 5.

3. "... a touching story about a boy and his love and devotion for a dog" (Paragraph 4)

   Tick (✔) the box beside the best definition of "touching" as it is used in this sentence.

exciting	
true	
fictional	
moving	

2 ■ 0

PAGE TOTAL

Marks

4. "... the almost impossible task ..." (Paragraph 5)

Why was Sue Potter's task so difficult?

_____ 2 1 0

Look at Paragraphs 6 to 8.

5. Write down any **three** qualities Celt needed to have if he was to become a film star.

_____

_____

_____ 2 1 0

Look at Paragraphs 9 to 11.

6. Tick (✔) the appropriate box to show whether the following statements are **True, False**, or **Cannot tell from the passage**.

	True	False	Cannot Tell
Sue trained Celt in Northern Ireland.			
Celt spent more time being filmed than being trained.			
Celt did well on the film set.			
Sue Potter owns two cats.			

2 ■ 0

2 ■ 0

2 ■ 0

2 ■ 0

7. Why does the writer use a **dash (—)** in the first sentence of Paragraph 10?

_____ 2 1 0

8. Write down an expression which suggests that Celt had been very well cared for during filming.

_____ 2 ■ 0

[Turn over

PAGE
TOTAL

Marks

Look at Paragraphs 12 to 14.

9. Give **three** reasons why Philip Daubeny was a suitable person to rescue Celt.

_____

_____

_____

2 | 1 | 0

Look at Paragraphs 15 to 18.

10. ". . . , Claire Millar, was working as a teacher with the children on the film."
    (Paragraph 15)

    Why do you think the children on the film needed a teacher?

    _____

    2 | 1 | 0

11. (a) Why was Philip Daubeny concerned for the safety of his cats?

    _____

    _____

    2 | 1 | 0

    (b) "I didn't want some terrible tragedy to happen with my five cats."
         (Paragraph 17)

         Identify **two** techniques used in this sentence to emphasise his concern.

    _____

    2 | 1 | 0

    (c) Do you think "tragedy" is a good word to use here? Give a reason.

    _____

    2 | ■ | 0

PAGE
TOTAL

Marks

12. ". . . had been living with cats in a temporary home . . ." (Paragraph 18)

Tick (✓) the box beside the best definition of "temporary" as it is used in this sentence.

long-lasting	
short-term	
animal	
caring	

2 ■ 0

Look at Paragraphs 19 to 22.

13. Give **two** pieces of evidence which show how Celt "fitted in very easily". (Paragraph 21)

_____

_____

2 1 0

14. What might some people find surprising about greyhounds?

_____

_____

2 1 0

Look at Paragraphs 23 to 27.

15. How does the structure of the sentence in Paragraph 25 emphasise Celt's good points?

_____

2 ■ 0

16. Why was the young boy in the film unable to adopt Celt?

_____

2 1 0

[Turn over for Questions 17 to 19 on *Page six*

PAGE
TOTAL

Marks

17. In what way had Celt "fallen on his feet" (Paragraph 27)?

_____

_____

2 1 0

Think about the passage as a whole.

18. Who do you think this passage is written for? Tick (✓) **one** box.

Film students	
Vets	
General readers	
Dog breeders	

2 ■ 0

19. "Why dumped dog is such a lucky hound"

Identify **two** techniques which help to make this a good title.

_____

_____

2 1 0

[END OF QUESTION PAPER]

PAGE
TOTAL

[BLANK PAGE]

G

0860/403

NATIONAL QUALIFICATIONS 2007	TUESDAY, 1 MAY 1.00 PM – 1.50 PM	**ENGLISH** STANDARD GRADE General Level Reading Text

Read carefully the passage overleaf. It will help if you read it twice. When you have done so, answer the questions. Use the spaces provided in the Question/Answer booklet.

SCOTTISH QUALIFICATIONS AUTHORITY

©

Biker Boys and Girls

There is only one "wall of death" doing the rounds at British fairs today. But a new generation of daredevil riders is intent on keeping the show on (or rather, off) the road.

1 Last year Kerri Cameron, aged 19 and a little bored with her job as a horse-riding instructor, was looking up job vacancies on the internet. Puzzled, she turned to her mother and said, "Mum, what's a wall of death?"

2 Her mother, Denise, a health worker who has always had a horror of motorcycles, told her that walls of death were places where people rode motorbikes round the insides of a 20 ft-high wooden drum and tried not to fall off and get killed. "Gosh," said Kerri, "that sounds fun."

3 She picked up her mobile, phoned the number mentioned on the internet and then arranged to see Ken Fox, owner of the wall of death. Ken Fox didn't ask about her school qualifications, only if she wanted a ride on the back of his bike around the wall. Yes, she said.

4 Ken Fox revved up the demonstration bike and spun it on to the 45-degree wooden apron that bridges the ground and the perpendicular wall and then took it three or four times around the lower bits of the wall itself just to see if she could cope. Then he went round with Kerri sitting on the handlebars. She passed that test, too. She thought it was fantastic. Unbelievable. The best!

5 A year later Kerri is doing 20 shows a day, driving a skeletal aluminium go-kart around Ken Fox's wall of death to within six inches of the safety wire at the top—the wire that's there to prevent the machines sailing off into the crowd. "It's much more fun than helping kids on horses," she says, giggling nervously and brushing a strand of blonde hair back behind her ear. "The only thing I really miss about home is flush toilets."

6 Ken Fox and his wife Julie, their sons, Luke and Alex, and their troupe of Kerri, a new girl rider called Emma Starr, a man who prefers to be known just as Philip, and a wall-of-death enthusiast of an accountant named Neil Calladine, now operate the last wall of death in business in Britain. Calladine is the wall's "spieler", stalking the front of the attraction

with a microphone, promising thrills and excitement as Ken and Luke Fox sit on their bikes, creating the roaring throttle noises of impending danger. Later, Luke and his father dip and zig-zag their bikes across each other, spinning round the drum every four seconds, as the holiday crowds peer tentatively down over the safety wire and then, in the traditional way, shower coins into the ring after being told that wall-of-death riders can never get insurance. Each show lasts 20 minutes; at one stage four riders are zipping up, down and all around.

7 In the 1930s and 1940s there were almost 30 walls of death at seaside resorts and fairgrounds around the country, often competing side-by-side in fairgrounds; now there are four left. One is in a steam museum in Derbyshire, another is the hobby/toy of a Cornish builder, and a third is owned by a 54-year-old agricultural engineer who "has done everything in motorcycles except ridden a wall of death". That wall's old owner, Graham Cripsey, of the Cripsey fairground family, is coming down from Skegness to teach him how to ride it.

8 Only Ken Fox and his band, together with pet dog Freebie, two ferrets and two cockatiels, tour in the traditional way, squelching out of their winter quarters from behind the Cambridgeshire hedgerows just before Easter and heading in convoy for the first of the 6,000 miles they will complete by the end of October. Ken is lucky that Julie can drive one of the trucks, change the 2 ft-high tyres, make sure Alex does his school lessons on his laptop, cook, make sandwiches and dish out the £2 tickets. She, too, loves the travelling life. "When you think I used to be a dental nurse," she says, her eyes misting a little.

9 She also helped her husband build his wall of death. "My old wall was wearing out," he says, "so I bought a 200 ft section of very long,

very straight, Oregon pine that cost £70,000 (Oregon pine, one of the tallest trees in the world, is used for all walls of death because of the straightness of its grain and the lack of knot in its timber). I got the planks cut in a milling yard. I went to a boatyard where they built submarines. The place was so big we could have built 50 walls of death."

10   The motorbikes used for shows are Indian Scouts made in the 1920s by the Hendee Motorcycle Company of Springfield, Massachusetts, deliberately engineered for easy balance with all the controls on the left, so Chicago cops could use their right hands for drawing their revolvers and shooting at Al Capone-style gangsters. This means the bikes are perfect for tricks. Take your hand off the throttle of a modern motorbike and it slips back to idling mode, thus losing the power that keeps the bike on the wall. Take your hand off the throttle of an Indian Scout, and the revs stay as they are—which means that you can zoom round and round the wall of death, arms in the air, to your heart's content.

11   The first wall of death is said by Graham Cripsey to have come to Britain from America in 1928 with others close on its heels. His grandfather, Walter, and father, Roy, trained lions to ride in the sidecars, as did the famous George "Tornado" Smith at Southend's Kursaal fairground. The Cripseys also developed a technique of being towed round behind the Indian Scouts on roller skates. "If you were competing side by side in a fairground, you always had to have one stunt better than the other," explains Graham. Smith also kept a skeleton in a sidecar which, with a flick on a control, would suddenly sit bolt upright. And Ricky Abrey, 61, who rode with him as "The Black Baron", says Tornado perfected a ride where three riders would cut off their engines at the top of the wall and instantly re-start them again, causing the audience to gasp as 2 ft-long flashes of flame escaped the exhaust pipes.

12   Fun, then, for all the family. "People still love the wall of death," says Ken Fox emphatically. "People like what we put on and get good value for it. If they see it once, they always want to see it again. The problem is finding the people to work on it. There are a lot of soft men around."

13   "Wall of death" is, thankfully, a bit of a misnomer, for there have been no fatal accidents on British walls, though whether that's due to good luck or fear-induced careful preparation is difficult to tell. "I've been

knocked off by other riders, the engine's stalled, I've had punctures and I've hit a safety cable," says Ken Fox, pointing at his scars. "Everyone gets falls at some time but we try to be spot-on in our preparations. Before every show we spend a complete day trying to get the machines working perfectly."

14   Luke Fox suffered his first bad fall last year, flicking a safety-cable bolt on one of his "dips" as he zig-zagged his bike up and down. He fell 20 ft, got up and started again, even though he'd severely torn his knee. In a sense, he's got his own good-luck charm. His Indian bike was originally ridden by no less a daredevil than Tornado Smith himself. Luke has also inherited his father's total dedication to the trade and the Fox family wall looks set to last into the immediate future. Indeed, he and Kerri are now a partnership, sharing the long-haul driving and other things, while young Alex, the ferret-fancier, is raring for his first go at the wall.

15   Even Neil Calladine, the spieler, has shed his accountant duties and can indulge his lifelong passion for fairgrounds, though he needs to talk almost non-stop from 2 pm to 10 pm each show day and consumes mountains of throat sweets. "I make sure I go back and see the missus once a month," he says, "and of course I'm there all winter. I suppose I'm one of those fortunate people whose hobby has become his life. I love the freedom of travel, no nine-to-five, just us and the open road."

16   In that he's just like Kerri Cameron, bless her daredevil heart.

Adapted from an article
by John Dodd

[END OF PASSAGE]

[BLANK PAGE]

FOR OFFICIAL USE

G

Total
Mark

0860/404

NATIONAL
QUALIFICATIONS
2007

TUESDAY, 1 MAY
1.00 PM – 1.50 PM

ENGLISH
STANDARD GRADE
General Level
Reading
Questions

Fill in these boxes and read what is printed below.

Full name of centre

Town

Forename(s)

Surname

Date of birth
Day Month Year

Scottish candidate number

Number of seat

**NB Before leaving the examination room you must give this booklet to the invigilator.
If you do not, you may lose all the marks for this paper.**

SA 0860/404 6/75170

Marks

QUESTIONS

Write your answers in the spaces provided.

Look at Paragraphs 1 to 3.

1. **In your own words**, explain fully why Kerri Cameron was looking up job vacancies on the internet.

   _____

   2 1 0

2. What is surprising about Kerri's reaction to what her mother tells her about the wall of death?

   _____

   _____

   2 1 0

3. Why do you think Ken Fox was not interested in Kerri's school qualifications?

   _____

   _____

   2 ■ 0

Look at Paragraphs 4 and 5.

4. How does the writer suggest Kerri's enthusiasm after her test on the bike:

   (*a*) by word choice?

   _____

   2 ■ 0

   (*b*) by sentence structure?

   _____

   2 ■ 0

5. **Using your own words as far as possible**, describe **two** aspects of Kerri's performance which could be described as dangerous.

   _____

   _____

   2 1 0

PAGE
TOTAL

Marks

Look at Paragraph 6.

6. **In your own words**, explain the job of the "spieler".

_____

2 | 1 | 0

7. ". . . shower coins into the ring . . ."

Give **two** reasons why "shower" is an effective word to use in this context.

_____

_____

2 | 1 | 0

8. Why do you think members of the audience are told that wall-of-death riders "can never get insurance"?

_____

2 | ■ | 0

9. Explain fully what the expression "zipping up, down and all around" suggests about the riders' performance.

_____

_____

2 | 1 | 0

Look at Paragraphs 7 to 9.

10. How does the writer illustrate the decline in popularity of walls of death?

_____

2 | 1 | 0

[Turn over

PAGE TOTAL

Marks

11. "Only Ken Fox and his band . . ." (Paragraph 8)

Write down **one** word from earlier in the passage which contains the same idea as "band".

```
┌─────────────────────────────┐
│                             │
│                             │
└─────────────────────────────┘
```

2 ■ 0

12. Explain fully why you think the writer uses the word "squelching" in Paragraph 8.

_____

_____

2 1 0

13. Look again at the sentence which begins "Ken is lucky . . ." (Paragraph 8).

How does the structure of the **whole** sentence help to reinforce how busy Julie is between Easter and October?

_____

_____

2 1 0

14. Why is Oregon pine so suitable for walls of death?

_____

2 1 0

Look at Paragraph 10.

15. **Using your own words as far as possible**, explain why the Indian Scout bikes are "perfect for tricks."

_____

_____

2 1 0

PAGE
TOTAL

Marks

16. **Identify two techniques** used by the writer which help to involve the reader in his description of the Indian Scout motorbikes. **Quote evidence** from the paragraph to support your answers.

Technique	Evidence

2 1 0

2 1 0

Look at Paragraphs 11 and 12.

17. Why might the nicknames "Tornado" and "The Black Baron" be suitable for wall-of-death riders?

Tornado

_____

The Black Baron

_____

2 1 0

[Turn over

PAGE
TOTAL

Marks

18. (*a*) Write down **four** things the early wall-of-death riders included in their acts.

_____

_____

_____

_____ **2 1 0**

(*b*) **In your own words**, give **two** reasons why such things were included in the acts.

_____

_____ **2 1 0**

Look at Paragraphs 13 to 16.

19. ". . . is, thankfully, a bit of a misnomer, . . ." (Paragraph 13)

(*a*) Tick (✓) the box beside the best definition of "misnomer".

old-fashioned attraction	
risky venture	
successful show	
wrongly applied name	

(*b*) Write down evidence from the passage to support your answer to 19(*a*).

_____ **2 1 0**

20. Why is the word "dips" (Paragraph 14) in inverted commas?

_____ **2 ■ 0**

PAGE
TOTAL

Marks

21. Give **three** pieces of evidence to support the writer's statement that "the Fox family wall looks set to last into the immediate future" (Paragraph 14).

_____

_____

_____ 2 1 0

22. Show how the final paragraph is an effective conclusion to this article.

_____

_____ 2 1 0

[END OF QUESTION PAPER]

PAGE
TOTAL

FOR OFFICIAL USE

p2	
p3	
p4	
p5	
p6	
p7	
TOTAL MARK	

[BLANK PAGE]

F

0860/401

NATIONAL
QUALIFICATIONS
2008

TUESDAY, 6 MAY
10.35 AM – 11.25 AM

ENGLISH
STANDARD GRADE
Foundation Level
Reading
Text

Read carefully the passage overleaf. It will help if you read it twice. When you have done so, answer the questions. Use the spaces provided in the Question/Answer booklet.

SQA

Home for Christmas

1   Christmas Eve was not a good day to hitch-hike. Billy had been at the motorway services for nearly five hours without a sniff of a lift. No-one had even slowed down to take a look at him. And the weather was lousy. At one point, he'd had to shelter from the rain next to some bins behind the petrol station. He'd dozed off, and there was another hour gone.

2   Now it was getting dark, and a fog was coming in. Cars drove by him as if he wasn't there. So much for Christmas spirit! It wasn't as though Billy had a big, off-putting bag either. All he carried was a small rucksack, which used to belong to his mum. It contained all his worldly goods, such as they were, and would fit beneath his legs in the smallest car.

3   Maybe he should cross the six-lane road, and try to hitch back to London, where he'd come from that morning. People said that you could get a bed and something to eat more easily at Christmas. But no. With Billy's luck, he'd probably get run over crossing the motorway.

4   Billy began to cough. He'd had this cold on and off for two months. Other homeless people told him that your body got used to the life, when you'd been living on the streets long enough. Maybe. He'd been sleeping rough for a year now. That was long enough for him to decide that it wasn't the life for him.

5   The fog was getting thicker. It was colder, too. When it got really dark, he'd wander into the café, warm up a bit. Billy had enough money left for a cup of coffee. That was, presuming they'd serve him. He looked a mess.

6   The rain started up again. Billy shivered. His jacket was supposed to be "shower-proof", but it was wet through. Puddles were forming around his feet. Suddenly, he saw a lorry, coming towards him from the direction of the petrol station. The lorry didn't have its lights on and was driving really close to the kerb. Instead of holding his thumb out, Billy took a step back. He didn't want to get splashed by the foul, oily water that lay on the road.

7   Still, the lorry seemed to be driving straight at him. Billy decided to get out of its way. But as he was about to make his move, the lorry turned its lights on, full beam. He couldn't see a thing. He stood there, frozen to the spot, like a rabbit dazzled by a poacher's torch, waiting to be shot.

8   The lorry stopped. One of its wheels was on the kerb, only centimetres from Billy's right foot. The passenger door opened. A deep voice spoke.

9   "You after a lift?"

10   It all felt wrong. Billy knew that. But it was raining hard now, and he had been there all day. He went up to the door and opened it a little farther.

11   "How far are you going?" the deep voice asked.

12   Billy still couldn't see the driver, only hear his harsh voice.

13   "I'm going to Scotland. To Gretna."

14   "I'm going that way myself. Get in."

15   Billy hesitated. He had learnt to walk away from threatening situations. But the man's accent was Scottish, like his, and he could take him all the way home—or, at least, to the place he used to call home.

16   Billy got into the cabin. He slid his bag beneath his feet and pulled on the seatbelt before looking at the driver.

17   "Thanks for stopping," he said. "It's pretty horrible out there."

18   The man said nothing. His thick hands reached for the gear stick. He began to accelerate onto the M1, towards the grim, frozen north.

19   In the half light of the lorry cabin, Billy looked at the driver. The man was in his late thirties, forty at most. He had short, dark hair. His eyes were set so deeply beneath his heavy eyebrows that Billy could barely make them out. His face was scarred. He was heavy set and wore a lumberjack shirt over shapeless jeans.

20   Billy hadn't done a lot of hitching, but he knew that there was an etiquette. The hitcher had to make conversation. It was your duty to entertain the driver, even if he didn't have a lot to say for himself. The driver had to concentrate on the driving, after all.

21   "I'm Billy," he said to the man, in his friendliest voice, "Billy Gates."

22   For a moment, he thought that the driver wasn't going to reply.

23   "Hank."

24   "Bad day to have to work, Christmas Eve."

25   Again, Hank didn't answer. Instead, he speeded up, until they were doing fifty. The fog was getting thicker and it felt too fast. Still, it wasn't Billy's place to say their speed was dangerous.

26   The silence was almost as threatening as the speed they were doing. There was a radio. Billy wondered whether he should suggest switching it on.

27   "Should I . . . ?"

28   Hank interrupted before Billy had formed the sentence.

29   "I don't like music."

30   The way he said it made Billy want to jump out of the cab, even though their speed was up to fifty-five and there was nothing but filthy fog outside. Instead, he began to say the first things that came into his mind.

31   "Do you know how many cars went by before you picked me up?"

32   Hank remained silent.

33   "A thousand at least."

34   Now that he'd starting talking, he couldn't stop.

35   "I think this time of year is a pain, really," Billy said. "You know what I mean? Everyone's expected to have a good time, so when you're not, somehow it seems a hundred times worse."

36   "Aye," said Hank. "I know that all right."

37   He began to drive even faster.

Adapted from a short story

[END OF PASSAGE]

[BLANK PAGE]

FOR OFFICIAL USE

F

Total Mark

0860/402

NATIONAL QUALIFICATIONS 2008

TUESDAY, 6 MAY 10.35 AM – 11.25 AM

ENGLISH STANDARD GRADE Foundation Level Reading Questions

Fill in these boxes and read what is printed below.

Full name of centre

Town

Forename(s)

Surname

Date of birth
Day Month Year

Scottish candidate number

Number of seat

NB Before leaving the examination room you must give this booklet to the invigilator. If you do not, you may lose all the marks for this paper.

SQA

Marks

QUESTIONS

Write your answers in the spaces provided.

Look at Paragraphs 1 and 2.

1. **When** and **where** does the story begin?

_____

_____   **2 1 0**

2. ". . . not a good day to hitch-hike." (Paragraph 1)

    Give **two** pieces of evidence from Paragraph 1 which show this is true.

    (i) _____

    (ii) _____   **2 1 0**

3. Billy's situation becomes worse as it grows late.

    Write down two things from Paragraph 2 which add to his difficulties.

    (i) _____

    (ii) _____   **2 1 0**

4. **Write down an expression** from Paragraph 2 which shows that drivers paid no attention to Billy.

    _____   **2 ■ 0**

5. Billy is carrying a rucksack.

    Why would this **not** be a problem for drivers?

    _____   **2 ■ 0**

PAGE
TOTAL

Marks

6. Give **two** reasons why the rucksack might be important to Billy.

_____

_____   2 1 0

Look at Paragraphs 3 to 5.

7. Billy thinks about crossing the road and returning to London.

   (*a*)   Why does he consider doing this?

   _____

   _____   2 1 0

   (*b*)   Why does he decide **not** to?

   _____   2 ■ 0

8. Billy is in bad physical shape.

   (*a*)   **Write down two ways** the writer shows us this.

   _____   2 1 0

   (*b*)   **Why** is Billy in such bad shape?

   _____   2 1 0

9. Give **two** reasons why Billy plans to go into the café later.

   (i) _____

   (ii) _____   2 1 0

10. **Write down an expression** which suggests he is a bit unsure about going into the café.

   _____   2 ■ 0

[Turn over

PAGE
TOTAL

Marks

Look at Paragraphs 6 and 7.

11. The weather is making Billy more and more miserable.

Write down three things which show this.

(i) _____

(ii) _____

(iii) _____ 2 1 0

12. **Why** has the writer put inverted commas around the word "shower-proof"?

_____ 2 ■ 0

13. When Billy **first** sees the lorry (Paragraph 6), which **two** things make it dangerous?

(i) _____

(ii) _____ 2 1 0

14. ". . . like a rabbit dazzled by a poacher's torch, waiting to be shot." (Paragraph 7)

(*a*) What technique is the writer using in this expression? Tick (✓) the correct box.

rhyme	
metaphor	
alliteration	
simile	

2 ■ 0

(*b*) What **two** things does this expression suggest about Billy?

(i) _____

(ii) _____ 2 1 0

PAGE
TOTAL

Marks

Look at Paragraphs 8 to 18.

15. **Before** Billy gets into the lorry, how does the writer make the driver seem mysterious and threatening?

_____

2 | 1 | 0

16. "Billy hesitated." (Paragraph 15)

Give **two** reasons why he then decides to accept the lift after all.

(i) _____

(ii) _____

2 | 1 | 0

17. ". . . —or, at least, to the place he used to call home." (Paragraph 15)

How do you think Billy feels about his home in Scotland?

_____

2 | ■ | 0

18. ". . . the grim, frozen north." (Paragraph 18)

Explain why this is a good description of Billy's destination.

_____

2 | 1 | 0

Look at Paragraphs 19 and 20.

19. ". . . etiquette." (Paragraph 20)

Tick (✓) the box beside the best definition of "etiquette".

a conversation	
a gadget	
a way of behaving correctly	
a solution to a problem	

2 | ■ | 0

[Turn over for Questions 20 to 22 on *Page six*

PAGE
TOTAL

Marks

Look at Paragraphs 21 to 37.

20. Billy becomes more and more nervous.

Write down three things about Hank's behaviour which make Billy feel like this.

(i) _____

(ii) _____

(iii) _____ 2 1 0

21. "Everyone's expected to have a good time . . ." (Paragraph 35)

Why does this bother Billy?

_____

_____ 2 1 0

Think about the passage as a whole.

22. Do you feel sorry for Billy?

Tick (✓) **one** box.

Yes [ ]

No [ ]

Give **two** reasons from the passage to support your answer.

(i) _____

_____

(ii) _____

_____ 2 1 0

[END OF QUESTION PAPER]

PAGE
TOTAL

FOR OFFICIAL USE

p2 ☐

p3 ☐

p4 ☐

p5 ☐

p6 ☐

TOTAL
MARK ☐

[BLANK PAGE]

[BLANK PAGE]

G

0860/403

NATIONAL
QUALIFICATIONS
2008

TUESDAY, 6 MAY
1.00 PM – 1.50 PM

ENGLISH
STANDARD GRADE
General Level
Reading
Text

Read carefully the passage overleaf. It will help if you read it twice. When you have done so, answer the questions. Use the spaces provided in the Question/Answer booklet.

✕✕SQA

Saddle the white horses

Thurso prepares to host its first professional surf tour, confirming Scotland's status as a world–class surfing destination.

1 It was the stickers that gave it away. Turning left on the A9 at Latheron in Caithness, you were suddenly faced with a sign that looked as though it had been defaced by advertising executives from surfing companies. Like a cairn on a mountain path, the big green board declaring Thurso to be 23 miles away told travelling bands of surfers that they'd taken the right turn-off and were nearly at their destination. Slapping another sticker on the sign was like laying another stone on the pile.

2 Thurso is about to enter surfing's big league.

3 It's hard to reconcile the popular tropical imagery of surfing with the town, a raw, exposed kind of place that enjoys little escape from the worst excesses of the Scottish climate. The Caithness coastline is peppered with surfing spots, but the jewel in the crown and the target for dedicated wave riders lies within spitting distance of Thurso town centre at a reef break called Thurso East. In the right conditions, the swell there rears up over kelp-covered slabs into a fast-moving, barrelling monster of a wave considered world class by those in the know.

4 Now Thurso East is the focus of a huge professional surfing tour. The week-long Highland Open marks the first time a World Qualifying Series (WQS) surfing competition has been held in Scotland. It will also be the furthest north a WQS tour has ever travelled, anywhere in the world.

5 Professional competitive surfing has two tours: the WQS and the World Championship Tour (WCT). The WCT is the premier division, with the WQS being used as a platform for professionals to move up into the big time. Around 160 up-and-coming wave riders are expected to take part in the Thurso event. Prize money of $100,000 (£57,000) is up for grabs, along with vital tour points.

6 "Travelling and exploring new places is part of the whole surfing culture," says Bernhard Ritzer, the Highland Open event manager. "We've had so much feedback from surfers from Australia and Brazil who want to go. They see it as an adventure and as something new. We did a photo trip there last year with some of our team riders and they were impressed. They're excited about it—although it will still be a shock because I don't think they know how cold and harsh it can be."

7 "Thurso is one of the best waves in Europe, if not the world," he says. "Most people don't even know it, and it's just so good. It doesn't always have to be sunny, warm and tropical. It can also be cold, rough and hard.

8 "The idea is to have a contrast to the summer events in the tropical islands. We also have something in the north to show that this is part of surfing. Very often on the WQS tour the waves aren't that good, but here they are expecting big reef break waves and they like to surf those."

9 Surfers generally guard their local breaks jealously. It's considered essential to keep your mouth shut about your "secret spot", in case you find it overrun with visitors. So, economic benefits to Thurso aside, some local surfers were a little concerned about an event on this scale descending on their area. WQS representatives met with these surfers to address their concerns and feel that they've pretty much got everyone on board. WQS is also paying for improvements to the car parking area near the Thurso East break.

10 "We're concerned to get the locals involved," says Ritzer. "We want to keep them happy and don't want to look too commercial, coming in with a big event machine. We need them to help organise local stuff. You always have some individuals who will boycott everything, but we understand that most of them are positive."

14   Robertson, 23, who has been surfing since he was four, criss-crosses the globe with his fellow WQS competitors in pursuit of the best waves and a place on the coveted WCT tour. He may as well be going to surf on the moon for all he knows about Thurso East, but that's part of the appeal.

15   "We follow the surf around all year and go to a lot of different places, but Scotland's somewhere probably none of us have been to," he says. "That for me was a big part of wanting to go, to see the place. As a professional surfer, you've got to live out of your bag a lot, travelling around with long stints away from home, but when you perform well in the event or get some really good waves, it makes it all worth it.

16   "I feel pretty good and I'm hoping to do well," he adds. "Everyone who does the tour is feeling good too, so it should be a great event. It'll be interesting to see what the waves are like."

17   Competitors will be scored by a team of eight international judges on the length of their ride, the difficulty of moves and how they connect it all together. Waves are scored on a one to ten scale, with ten a perfect ride, and the final scores are based on each surfer's two highest-scoring waves.

18   "These events raise the profile of locations, create investment in areas and hopefully provide opportunities for young surfers coming through to grow and compete at world-class levels," says Dave Reed, contest director for the WQS event. "It's a great way to say we've got some of the best waves in the world."

Adapted from a magazine article

[END OF PASSAGE]

11   Andy Bain probably knows the break at Thurso East better than anyone, although he'll be watching the competition from the shoreline. Bain, who runs Thurso Surf, has been surfing the reef there for 17 years and is eagerly anticipating the arrival of the Highland Open. He's aware of the concerns and the possible exposure of his home break, but doesn't anticipate a negative impact.

12   "From the surf school side of things it's good because it'll generate business for us," says Bain, 33. "As a local surfer, it's kind of like closure for me to have this competition. To say the world has now recognised Thurso as a top surfing destination makes me feel proud. A lot of people say it's going to get crowded and exposed, but with it being a cold destination I don't think it's going to be that bad."

13   For professional surfer Adam Robertson from Victoria, Australia, the trip to Thurso will be something of a journey into the unknown. "This will be the first time I've ever been to Scotland," says Robertson, who has competed on the WQS tour for the past three years. "We're all a bit worried about how cold it's going to be. Apart from that we're pretty excited because it's a place we've never been."

[BLANK PAGE]

FOR OFFICIAL USE

G

Total
Mark

0860/404

NATIONAL
QUALIFICATIONS
2008

TUESDAY, 6 MAY
1.00 PM – 1.50 PM

ENGLISH
STANDARD GRADE
General Level
Reading
Questions

Fill in these boxes and read what is printed below.

Full name of centre

Town

Forename(s)

Surname

Date of birth
Day Month Year

Scottish candidate number

Number of seat

**NB Before leaving the examination room you must give this booklet to the invigilator.
If you do not, you may lose all the marks for this paper.**

✕SQA

QUESTIONS

Write your answers in the spaces provided.

Look at Paragraphs 1 to 3.

1. (*a*) What had been added to the road sign in Caithness?

_____

| | 2 | ■ | 0 |

(*b*) Write down **two** things the surfers would know when they saw this road sign.

_____

_____

| | 2 | 1 | 0 |

2. "Thurso is about to enter surfing's big league." (Paragraph 2)

How does the writer make this statement stand out?

_____

| | 2 | ■ | 0 |

3. Thurso is different from the popular image of a surfing location.

(*a*) **In your own words**, describe the popular image of a surfing location.

_____

| | 2 | ■ | 0 |

(*b*) **Write down an expression** showing how Thurso is different.

_____

| | 2 | ■ | 0 |

4. What do the words "jewel in the crown" (Paragraph 3) suggest about Thurso East?

_____

| | 2 | ■ | 0 |

5. "... a fast-moving, barrelling monster ..." (Paragraph 3)

Explain fully why this is an effective description of the wave.

_____

_____

| | 2 | 1 | 0 |

Marks

PAGE
TOTAL

Marks

Look at Paragraphs 4 and 5.

6. In which **two** ways is the Highland Open different from other WQS surfing competitions?

    (i) _____

    (ii) _____   2 | 1 | 0

7. **In your own words**, explain the difference between the two professional surfing tours.

    WCT _____

    WQS _____   2 | 1 | 0

8. Which **two** benefits will the winner of the competition gain?

    (i) _____

    (ii) _____   2 | 1 | 0

Look at Paragraphs 6 to 8.

9. Give **three** reasons why, according to Bernhard Ritzer, surfers will want to visit Thurso.

    (i) _____

    (ii) _____

    (iii) _____   2 | 1 | 0

10. According to Ritzer, what will surprise the surfers?

    _____   2 | ■ | 0

[Turn over

Marks

11. Thurso can offer something which many other surfing locations cannot.

What is this?

_____

2 ■ 0

Look at Paragraphs 9 and 10.

12. "Surfers generally guard their local breaks . . . " (Paragraph 9)

In your own words, explain why surfers do this.

_____

2 1 0

13. What **style** of language is used in the expression "keep your mouth shut" (Paragraph 9)?

_____

2 ■ 0

14. Which **two key** things have WQS representatives done to gain support?

(i) _____

(ii) _____

2 1 0

15. The WQS representatives feel that "they've pretty much got everyone on board." (Paragraph 9)

Write down an expression from Paragraph 10 which continues this idea.

_____

2 ■ 0

16. **Write down a single word** from this section meaning "refuse to support or take part".

2 ■ 0

PAGE
TOTAL

Marks

Look at Paragraphs 11 to 18.

17. (*a*) How does local surfer Andy Bain feel about the competition?

Tick (✓) the best answer.

very negative and angry	
quite pleased but worried	
excited and not really anxious	

2 ■ 0

(*b*) **Write down an expression** to support your chosen answer.

_____

2 ■ 0

18. "He may as well be going to surf on the moon . . . " (Paragraph 14)

What does this comparison suggest about Thurso?

_____

2 ■ 0

19. In Paragraph 15, Australian Adam Robertson describes his life as a professional surfer.

In your own words, sum up the **negative** and **positive** aspects of his life.

(*a*) **negative:** _____

_____

2 1 0

(*b*) **positive:** _____

_____

2 1 0

20. What **three** elements of the surfers' performance are judged?

(i) _____

(ii) _____

(iii) _____

2 1 0

[Turn over

PAGE
TOTAL

Marks

Think about the passage as a whole.

21. (i) What do you think is the main purpose of this passage?

Tick (✓) **one** box.

to tell the reader some amusing stories about surfing	
to inform the reader about a surfing competition in Scotland	
to argue against holding a surfing competition in Scotland	

(ii) Give a reason to support your answer.

_____

_____

2 1 0

[END OF QUESTION PAPER]

PAGE
TOTAL

FOR OFFICIAL USE

p2	
p3	
p4	
p5	
p6	
TOTAL MARK	

[BLANK PAGE]

[BLANK PAGE]

**F
G
C**

0860/407

NATIONAL
QUALIFICATIONS
2006

WEDNESDAY, 3 MAY
9.00 AM – 10.15 AM

ENGLISH
STANDARD GRADE
Foundation, General
and Credit Levels
Writing

Read This First

1   Inside this booklet, there are photographs and words.
Use them to help you when you are thinking about what to write.
Look at all the material and think about all the possibilities.

2   There are 21 assignments altogether for you to choose from.

3   Decide which assignment you are going to attempt.
Choose only **one** and write its number in the margin of your answer book.

4   Pay close attention to what you are asked to write.
Plan what you are going to write.
Read and check your work before you hand it in.
Any changes to your work should be made clearly.

SCOTTISH
QUALIFICATIONS
AUTHORITY

FIRST **Look at the picture opposite.**
It shows a couple parting.

NEXT Think how you might feel about leaving someone you care for.

WHAT YOU HAVE TO WRITE
---

1. **Write about** a time when you were separated from someone you cared about.

    You should concentrate on your **thoughts and feelings**.

    OR

2. **Write a short story** using the title:

    Never Forgotten.

    OR

3. We should be less afraid to speak openly about our feelings.

    Discuss.

    OR

4. **Write in any way you choose** using the picture opposite as your inspiration.

[Turn over

FIRST   **Look at the picture opposite.
It shows a lightning strike.**

NEXT   Think about the power of storms.

WHAT YOU HAVE TO WRITE

5. **Describe** both the excitement and the fear you experienced when you were caught in a storm.

   OR

6. **Write a short story** using **ONE** of the following titles:

   Stormchaser   Lightning Strikes Twice.

   OR

7. **Write a newspaper article** with the following headline:

   Storm Causes Widespread Damage.

   OR

8. Weather plays an important part in our everyday lives.

   Give your views.

[Turn over

FIRST   **Look at the picture opposite.
          It shows a group of students.**

NEXT   Think about life during and after school.

    WHAT YOU HAVE TO WRITE

---

   9. **Giving reasons**, write about your plans for when you leave school.

       OR

   10. **Write a short story** using the following title:

       The Examination.

       OR

   11. **Write an article** for your school magazine in which you describe
       the high points **and** the low points of your school years.

       OR

   12. New places, new faces.

       Write about a time when you had to cope with new people in new
       surroundings.

       Remember to include your **thoughts and feelings**.

                                                              [Turn over

FIRST **Look at the picture opposite.**
It shows a traffic jam.

NEXT Think about travel problems.

WHAT YOU HAVE TO WRITE

13. **Write about** an occasion when you were delayed during a journey.
You should concentrate on your **thoughts and feelings**.

OR

14. **Write a short story** using the following title:
The Road to Nowhere.

OR

15. Road rage, air rage—the modern age.
Life today is simply too stressful.
Discuss.

[Turn over

FIRST **Look at the picture opposite.**
It shows a young couple who have fallen out.

NEXT Think about relationships.

WHAT YOU HAVE TO WRITE

16. **Write a short story** using **ONE** of the following openings:

EITHER

Jill stared ahead intently, always away from him, focused firmly on the wall. He tried to speak. She raised her arm in protest . . .

OR

Andrew didn't know what to do. Just hours earlier things had been simply perfect. Now this. He let his mind wander back to . . .

OR

17. Magazines for young people do more good than harm.

Give your views.

OR

18. **Write about** your **thoughts and feelings** at a time when you were aware that someone simply wasn't listening.

[Turn over for assignments 19 to 21 on *Page twelve*

There are no pictures for these assignments.

19. **Write a short story** using the following opening.

    "He awoke in the ashes of a dead city. The cruel sun glared, showing neither pity nor mercy. He shook himself. It was no dream."

    Make sure that you develop **character** and **setting** as well as **plot**.

    OR

20. Look at me!

    Is it more important to be an individual or to fit in with the crowd?

    Discuss.

    OR

21. **Write a short story** using the title:

    Out of Time.

    Make sure that you develop **character** and **setting** as well as **plot**.

[END OF QUESTION PAPER]

[BLANK PAGE]

F G C

0860/407

NATIONAL QUALIFICATIONS 2007	TUESDAY, 1 MAY 9.00 AM – 10.15 AM	**ENGLISH STANDARD GRADE** Foundation, General and Credit Levels Writing

Read This First

1 Inside this booklet, there are photographs and words.
   Use them to help you when you are thinking about what to write.
   Look at all the material and think about all the possibilities.

2 There are 23 assignments altogether for you to choose from.

3 Decide which assignment you are going to attempt.
   Choose only **one** and write its number in the margin of your answer book.

4 Pay close attention to what you are asked to write.
   Plan what you are going to write.
   Read and check your work before you hand it in.
   Any changes to your work should be made clearly.

SCOTTISH
QUALIFICATIONS
AUTHORITY
©

SA 0860/407 6/75170

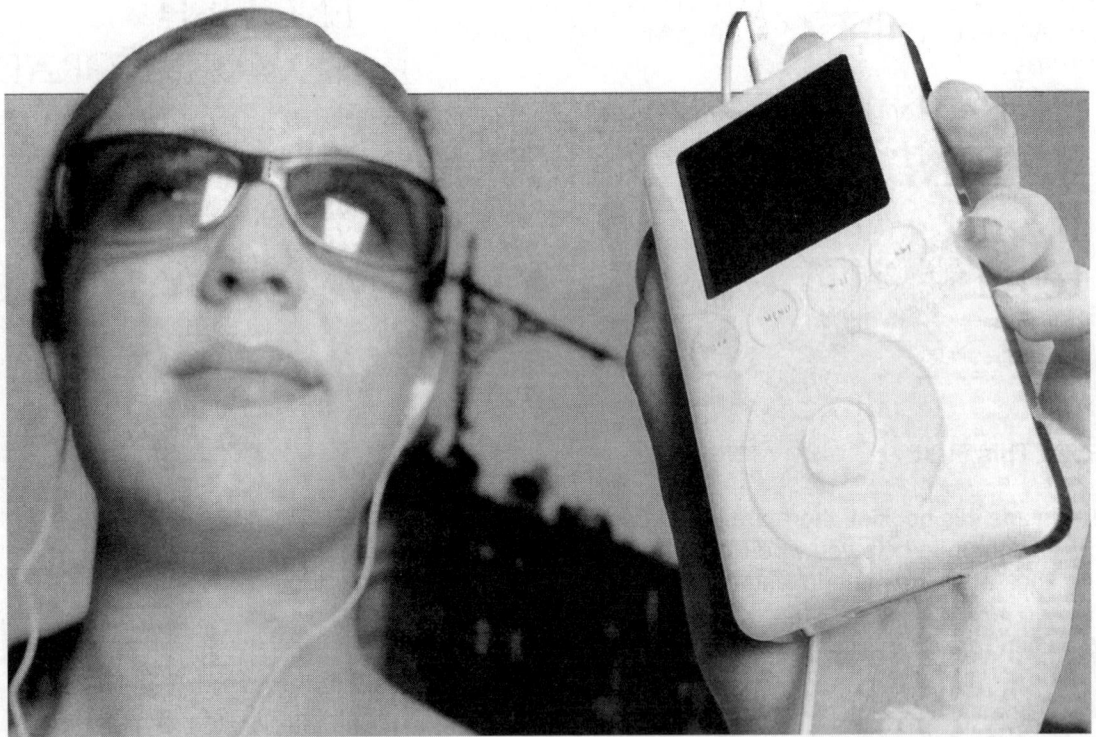

FIRST   **Look at the picture opposite.
It shows a young woman with an MP3 player.**

NEXT   Think about the importance of technology.

WHAT YOU HAVE TO WRITE

1. The one piece of technology I couldn't live without.
   Write about the importance to you of **ONE** piece of technology.

   OR

2. Young people today care too much for personal possessions.
   Give your views.

   OR

3. **Write a short story** using **ONE** of the following titles:

   Futureshock   She Saw the Future.

   You should develop **setting** and **character** as well as **plot**.

   [Turn over

FIRST   **Look at the picture opposite.
It shows a young boy being led by his mother.**

NEXT   Think about your schooldays.

> WHAT YOU HAVE TO WRITE

4. School Memories.

   Write about a person, place, or incident from your schooldays which you find unforgettable.

   Remember to include your **thoughts and feelings**.

   OR

5. **Write a short story** using the following opening:

   The reluctance was written all over John's face. He tugged at his mother's hand. He winced. He grimaced. He complained. Still his mother led him on . . .

   You should develop **setting** and **character** as well as **plot**.

   OR

6. All pupils should wear school uniform.

   Give your views.

[Turn over

FIRST **Look at the picture opposite.**
It shows a lake in winter.

NEXT Think about special places.

WHAT YOU HAVE TO WRITE

7. Sometimes a special place can inspire us.

   Write about such a place.

   Remember to include your **thoughts and feelings**.

   OR

8. **Write in any way you choose** using the picture opposite as your inspiration.

   OR

9. **Write about** a time when you were alone but happy.

   You should concentrate on your **thoughts and feelings**.

   OR

10. **Write an informative article** for a travel magazine titled:

    The Best Holiday Destination For Young People.

[Turn over

FIRST   **Look at the picture opposite.
It shows a man under pressure.**

NEXT   Think about the pressures of life.

WHAT YOU HAVE TO WRITE

---

11. **Write about** a time in your life when you had to face personal pressure.

    You should describe your **thoughts and feelings**.

    OR

12. **Write a short story** using **ONE** of the following titles:

    The Underdog   Free at Last.

    You should develop **setting** and **character** as well as **plot**.

    OR

13. It's Just Not Fair!

    Write about an occasion when you took a stand against injustice.

    You should concentrate on your **thoughts and feelings** as well as what you did.

    OR

14. These days young people are unfairly treated by the media.

    Give your views.

                                                            [Turn over

FIRST   **Look at the picture opposite.**
             It shows a young woman on a bus, alone with her thoughts.

NEXT   Think about moments of reflection.

| WHAT YOU HAVE TO WRITE |

15. "The glass is always half full; never half empty."

    It is important to have a positive outlook on life.

    Give your views.

    OR

16. **Write about** an occasion when you had an unpleasant duty to perform.

    You should concentrate on your **thoughts and feelings**.

    OR

17. Act Your Age!

    There are fewer chances today simply to be yourself.

    Give your views.

    OR

18. **Write a short story** using **ONE** of the following titles:

    Stranger in a Strange Land   No Return.

    You should develop **setting** and **character** as well as **plot**.

                    [Turn over for assignments 19 to 23 on *Page twelve*

There are no pictures for these assignments.

19. We should try to solve the problems here on earth before we spend more on space exploration.

    Give your views.

    OR

20. **Describe the scene** brought to mind by the following:

    A stark land of leafless trees and merciless wind.

    OR

21. We forget our past at our peril!

    Not enough is being done to keep Scottish heritage alive.

    Write a newspaper article in which you give your views on this topic.

    OR

22. There are special times of the year when people celebrate in their own way.

    Describe such a special time, bringing out its importance to you, your family, and your community.

    OR

23. **Write a short story** using the following title:

    The Traveller.

    You should develop **setting** and **character** as well as **plot**.

[END OF QUESTION PAPER]

[BLANK PAGE]

F
G
C

0860/407

NATIONAL
QUALIFICATIONS
2008

TUESDAY, 6 MAY
9.00 AM – 10.15 AM

ENGLISH
STANDARD GRADE
Foundation, General
and Credit Levels
Writing

Read This First

1   Inside this booklet, there are photographs and words.
    Use them to help you when you are thinking about what to write.
    Look at all the material and think about all the possibilities.

2   There are 22 assignments altogether for you to choose from.

3   Decide which assignment you are going to attempt.
    Choose only **one** and write its number in the margin of your answer book.

4   Pay close attention to what you are asked to write.
    Plan what you are going to write.
    Read and check your work before you hand it in.
    Any changes to your work should be made clearly.

X SQA

FIRST   **Look at the picture opposite.
It shows a car in heavy rain and hail.**

NEXT   Think about the dangers of extreme weather.

WHAT YOU HAVE TO WRITE

1. **Write a short story** using the following opening:

    The car skidded violently. He struggled to regain control. Close to panic, he wrenched the steering wheel to the right . . .

    You should develop **setting** and **character** as well as **plot**.

    OR

2. What's going on with our weather?

    Individuals need to take steps to tackle climate change.

    Give your views.

    OR

3. Journeys can take unexpected turns.

    Write about an occasion when this happened to **you**.

    Remember to include your **thoughts and feelings**.

[Turn over

FIRST **Look at the picture opposite.**
It shows young people together in a school cafeteria.

NEXT Think about school experiences.

> WHAT YOU HAVE TO WRITE

4. A Best Friend Should Be . . .
   Write about the ideal qualities of a best friend.

   OR

5. Youth culture. There's no such thing.
   Give your views.

   OR

6. **Write about** an occasion when your loyalty to a friend was pushed to the limit.

   Remember to include your **thoughts and feelings**.

   OR

7. **Write a short story** using the following title:

   The School Gate.

   You should develop **setting** and **character** as well as **plot**.

[Turn over

FIRST **Look at the picture opposite.**
It shows a man staring.

NEXT Think about being observed.

WHAT YOU HAVE TO WRITE

8. Big Brother is Watching You!

   Write about an occasion when you felt that there was no escape from authority.

   Remember to include your **thoughts and feelings**.

   OR

9. **Write a short story** using **ONE** of the following titles:

   Seeing is Believing   Close Up

   You should develop **setting** and **character** as well as **plot**.

   OR

10. All You Need is an Audience.

    The media give young people the idea that success comes easily.

    Give your views.

[Turn over

FIRST **Look at the picture opposite. It shows a boy with his grandfather.**

NEXT Think about the positive relationship you have with an older relative.

WHAT YOU HAVE TO WRITE

---

11. **Write about** an occasion when you learned a valuable lesson from an older relative.

    Remember to include your **thoughts and feelings**.

    OR

12. **Write a short story** using the following opening:

    Those were the moments he loved most. Grandpa reading to him with that lilting voice telling stories of . . .

    You should develop **setting** and **character** as well as **plot**.

    OR

13. We do not give the older generation the respect they deserve.

    Give your views.

    OR

14. **Write in any way you choose** using the picture opposite as your inspiration.

[Turn over

FIRST   **Look at the picture opposite.**
It shows an aircraft in the sunset.

NEXT   Think about air travel.

WHAT YOU HAVE TO WRITE

15. The damage to the environment caused by aircraft outweighs the advantages of cheap air travel.

    Give your views.

    OR

16. **Write a short story** using **ONE** of the following titles:

    A New Beginning   Touchdown

    You should develop **setting** and **character** as well as **plot**.

    OR

17. **Write in any way you choose** using the picture opposite as your inspiration.

[Turn over for assignments 18 to 22 on *Page twelve*

There are no pictures for these assignments.

18. **Write an informative article** for your school magazine titled:

   Technology: the impact on my education.

   OR

19. Nowadays there is less freedom of choice.

   Give your views.

   OR

20. **Write a short story** with the following opening:

   Beth stared again at the square glow from the computer screen in disbelief. She was going to be reunited with her sister at long last. She could hardly wait . . .

   You should develop **setting** and **character** as well as **plot**.

   OR

21. Education is about what we learn both **inside** and **outside** the classroom.

   Give your views.

   OR

22. **Describe the scene** brought to mind by **ONE** of the following:

   EITHER

   Snow fell, the flimsiest drops of geometric perfection, lightly, gently onto the village rooftops.

   OR

   With merciless rage, the sun scorched the earth to brittle hardness.

[END OF QUESTION PAPER]

[BLANK PAGE]

[BLANK PAGE]

[BLANK PAGE]

[BLANK PAGE]

[BLANK PAGE]

Acknowledgements

Leckie and Leckie is grateful to the copyright holders, as credited, for permission to use their material:
The Mail on Sunday for the article 'Pucker way to kiss a hummingbird'
by Mark Carwardine (2004 General Reading paper p 2);
The BBC for a photograph (2004 General Reading paper p 2);
Getty Images for a photograph (2004 Writing paper p 2);
Getty Images for a photograph (2004 Writing paper p 8);
Camera Press, London, for a photograph by John Swannell (2004 Writing paper p 10);
The Sunday Times for the article 'Dazzling the Stars' by John Harlow (2005 General Reading paper p 2);
FreeFoto.com for a photograph (2005 Writing paper p 4);
The Scotsman for a photograph (2005 Writing paper p 6);
Ralph A. Clevenger/Corbis for a photograph, © Ralph A Clevenger/CORBIS (2005 Writing paper p 8); Telegraph Group Limited for the article 'Ain't No Mountain High Enough' by Deborah Netburn, taken from The Sunday Telegraph Magazine, 27 June 2004 (2006 Foundation Reading paper p 2);
Getty/Matthew Cavanaugh for the photograph '77th Scripps Howard Spelling Bee Enters Final Round' (2006 General Reading paper p 2);
The Scotsman for the photograph 'Scots will be squeezed out. Fee Refugees!' (2006 Writing paper p 6);
Design Pics Inc./Alamy for the photograph 'People' (2006 Writing paper p 10);
Express Newspapers for an article from The Sunday Express: 'Why dumped dog is such a lucky hound' by David Wigg (2007 Foundation Reading paper p 2);
Rex Features Ltd for the photograph 'iPod Generation' by Dan Callister (2007 Writing paper p 2);
Getty Images for a photograph (2007 Writing paper p 4);
Dan Heller for the photograph from www.danheller.com (2007 Writing paper p 6);
Getty Images for a photograph by David Hogsholt (2007 Writing paper p 10);
Telegraph Group Limited for the article 'The Fabulous Biker Boys (and Girls)' by John Dodd, taken from The Sunday Telegraph Magazine 28th August 2005 (2007 General Reading paper p 2);
Scholastic for an extract from 'Home for Christmas' by David Belbin (2008 Foundation reading Paper pp 2-3);
Scotland on Sunday for a photograph 'Chips are down' by Robert Perry (2008 Writing Paper p 4);
FreeFoto.com for the photo 'Airbus A320' by Ian Britton (2008 Writing Paper p 10).

The following companies have very generously given permission to reproduce their copyright material free of charge:
FreeFoto.com for 4 photographs (2003 Writing paper pp 2, 4, 8 & 10); Maurice Lacroix Ltd for an advertisement (2004 Writing paper p 4); Newsquest Media Group for a photograph (2004 Writing paper p 4);
News Team International for a photograph (2004 Writing paper p 6);
The House of Lochar Publishers for an extract from Think Me Back by Catherine Forde (2005 Foundation Reading paper pp 2-4);
Newsquest Media Group for a photograph 'high Hopes' (2005 Writing paper p 10);
TES Scotland for a photograph (2005 Writing paper p 10);
Penguin for an extract from You Don't Know Me by David Klass © David Klass (2006 General Reading paper pp 2-4);
Newsquest Media Group for the photograph 'Stretching the Nerves' by Kieran Dodds (2006 Writing paper p 8);
Steve Double for a photograph (2008 Writing Paper p 6);
www.bigfoto.com for a photograph (2008 Writing Paper p 2).

Pocket answer section for
SQA Foundation and General English
5 years' Reading and 3 years' Writing

© 2008 Scottish Qualifications Authority/Leckie & Leckie, All Rights Reserved
Published by Leckie & Leckie Ltd, 3rd Floor, 4 Queen Street, Edinburgh EH2 1JE
tel: 0131 220 6831, fax: 0131 225 9987, enquiries@leckieandleckie.co.uk, www.leckieandleckie.co.uk

English Foundation Level
Reading 2004

1. At some point

2. (the pale) light

3. a whisper calling his name
   OR
   it was a low hiss calling his name

4. (i) alert

   (ii) tense/hardly daring to breathe

5. To { show **or** / emphasise **or** / build up **or** / increase **or** / add more } { tension **or** / atmosphere **or** / drama **or** / sudden realisation }

6. He was sleeping
   OR
   He was (fast) asleep.

7. (i) Not to wake his brother

   (ii) Not to let the voice know he was listening

8. Red/light/glow of the (camp) fire

9. The { amount **or** / degree **or** / quality } of { wetness **or** / dampness **or** / light }

10. **Any three** from:
    - Small/old woman
    - (Peculiar) bonnet
    - (Long) shawl
    - A person but not a person

11. stared with all my might
    OR
    trying to make out something definite

12. There has been an accident

13. **Any three** from:
    - it was his name which had been called/used
    - it was he who was specially needed
    - he could tell his brother later
    - he wanted to find out more (by himself)

14. He had gone to bed with his clothes on

15. **Any two** from:
    - (so) sure
    - no other possibility
    - Yes, the voice was climbing towards the farm

16. He would not be seen **so easily**

17. now and again
    OR
    bobbing

18. **Any two** from:
    - Commas
    - Climax
    - Onomatopoeia
    - Long sentence
    - Reference to or quotation of words relating to movement and struggling
    - "Panting"
    - Uses lots of verbs
    - Use of "crouched"

19. { He felt **or** / He thought **or** / It was as if } { it was very strong **or** / he was covered (in it) **or** / he could hardly breathe **or** / he was going to be sick **or** / he recognised it }

20. { To lead him **or** / To bring him **or** / To take him } { to free the fox cub **or** / to lift the slab }

21. eccentric

22. (i) He could lift the slab/She couldn't lift it

    (ii) The brother might kill it

23. (i) snapped (its teeth)

    (ii) hissed (like a cat)

24. To **suggest** speed/how fast it moved/suddenness of movement.

25. **One of**:
    - **Animal lover/walker/rambler**. Evidence: wandering the hills (paragraph 23)/tracks round the tent/watched him hunting
    - **Ghost/apparition**. Evidence: she had completely disappeared
    - **Farmer's mother**: Evidence from paragraph 8

English General Level
Reading 2004

1. encouraged **OR** embarrassing

2. associated it with red flowers which they associated with nectar/food

3. suggests no proof/doubt

4. Both:
   - Beatty's Guest Ranch
   - (in the mountains of) South-East Arizona/Mexico border

5. One of:
   - Expression/term used by hummingbird watchers
   - That is what hummingbird watchers call them
   - It is a colloquialism/nickname/slang

6. **Any one** from: (including explanation)
   - **Use of list** - gives number/range of feeder locations.
   - **Inversion** - links, develops information from previous sentence.
   - **Parenthesis** - gives additional information.

7. mind-boggling

8. great speed
   AND
   moving in all directions/chaotically

9. (hovering with) immaculate precision
   OR
   experienced helicopter pilots
   OR
   both/complete expression

10. **Any two** from:
    - So many varieties
    - Speed of the movement
    - Constant changes of colour

11. One of:
    - He believes their behaviour is trivial/unimportant
    - He thinks they are childish
    - He thinks it is petty

12. (i) attraction/to show off

    (ii) survival/camouflage

13. The (different) **sound** of their **wings**

14. Allusion to proverb
    OR
    Shows closeness to the bird **AND** makes use of alliteration

15. **Any two** from:
    - Contrasting **small** and **large**
    - Contrasting **stationary** and **moving**
    - Contrasting **delicate** and **clumsy**

16. One of:
    - He was **amazed**
    - He felt it was **incredible**
    - He was **privileged**
    - It was **beyond his expectations**

17. Both:
    - A hummingbird (constantly) needs lots of food/nectar
    - Like a fast car - needs lots of fuel **OR** like a busy person - needs lots of food/energy.

18. Both:
    - Fierce/aggressive
    - Competitive/territorial

19. Need both to **identify** and **comment** e.g.
    - **Structure**: the position of "Dutifully" at the beginning of the sentence to emphasise he is following instructions/to emphasise his reluctance
      OR
    - **Punctuation**: the use of dots to suggest a pause
      OR
    - **Punctuation**: reference to list/commas to highlight number/sequence of actions.

20. (sat there for) an eternity

21. unexpected/had not expected it/taken aback/ surprised

22. Need both a valid **reference/example** and an **appropriate comment**. e.g. "A dress and high heels are optional" – a self-deprecating aside included solely to create a ridiculous image of the (male) writer in female clothing

23. Need both an **appropriate viewpoint/feeling** and a **quotation/texture reference** e.g. He was amazed and touched by it; "every bit as impressive as rubbing shoulders with mountain gorillas".

English Foundation Level
Reading 2005

1. (still) dreaming

2. moved house, flitted etc

3. Jenny always cried/usually cried/had cried in the old house/never stopped crying OR he found it comforting

4. (*a*) (i) it had been done at speed/quickly/in a hurry
        (ii) it was untidy/difficult to read

    (*b*) hurried

5. Any two of
    • muffled
    • shrill
    • piercing
    • louder

6. annoyed/displeased/tired of it
    (Any negative feeling)

7. (i) wanted to go to the toilet (on her own)

    (ii) to stop Jenny being sick

8. more hassle than twenty Petes (had ever been)

9. (i) short sentence

    (ii) exclamation mark

10. Any two of:
    • stopped crying
    • instantly
    • her body relaxed (lifts acceptable)

11. (You should) give Mum a break

12. expertly

13. to protect her/keep her safe
    from the cold/from falling

14. (i) size - lift or gloss

    (ii) belongings - lift or gloss

    (iii) daydream - lift or gloss
         sleepover - friends could stay the night

15. He remembered/realised
    where he was/he had no friends

16. despondently

17. (i) (like) a jungle

    (ii) unruly (grasses)

    (iii) ramshackle (brick building)

18. a football player

19. Yanked
    Frustration

20. (i) pinched face

    (ii) tired voice/shaky voice

    (iii) looked as if she was going to cry

21. Take her mind off the baby/to distract her/change the subject

22. (i) snapped/yammering/bitterness/for goodness' sake/slamming

    (ii) Do what you like/Won't make any difference to me/I don't sleep these days

    (iii) Someone in this family . . . etc/sigh

23. (i) (too) powerful/loud

    (ii) (too) close

24. Any two of
    • caring – for his little sister/reference to mother's feelings
    • imaginative – jungle, day dream, football
    • moody – no friends
    • sensitive – to mother's feelings and situation/crying voice at end of passage
    NB No mark for unsupported choice alone

English General Level
Reading 2005

1. 6 years of (yellowing) newspapers
    70 videos of their performances

2. (i) She has spent £3,000

    (ii) She has seen them 17 times

    (iii) She now thinks/believes the band recognises
    her (as an acquaintance if not a friend)

3. It suggests she targets/singles him out/she is
    focused

4. She isn't really (an acquaintance)/being ironic

5. • Reference to her anger/strength of feeling.
    • Reference to <u>having to</u> defend him

6. Surprised/Disapproving

7. (a) Relaxed

    (b) she freely admits/has never caused me
    problems/sees nothing odd in it/I am not
    missing out on anything

8. (i) "about a third of people suffer (from 'celebrity
    worship syndrome')" Gloss or quote

    (ii) "may affect our mood" Gloss or quote

    (iii) "affects their mental well-being" Gloss or
    quote

9. To involve the reader/make you think/introduce
    the debate/introduce the central idea of the
    passage

10. Alexander the Great

11. (cultural phenomenon) for centuries/more than
    2,000 years ago

12. • Some attempt to gloss: "hundreds of star
    images"
    • Some attempt to gloss some or all of
    "advertising . . . other forms" e.g. mass media etc.

13. cannot get enough/shows their
    need/desire/strength/intensity of feeling/addiction
    to etc.

14. To prove how famous David Beckham is
    OR To highlight the extent of celebrity culture
    OR For humour + suitable comment

15. The internet

16. • Some attempt to gloss "gauge personality" e.g.
    what kind of person
    • Some attempt to gloss "level of interest in
    celebrities" e.g. how interested you are in
    famous people

17. (i) It exists in America & UK

    (ii) They have plastic surgery/he gives an example
    of a person who has become Pierce Brosnan

18. To show/indicate/highlight/emphasise
    a change/the opposite argument/the good side

19. (fables once sought in) fairytales

20. They were first/leaders in their field

21. • Attempt to gloss "dietary regime" e.g. improve
    diet
    • Reference to being fitter/healthier/better at
    football/having improved attitude/commitment
    to football or sport in general

22. (a) feel good/better about yourself
    i.e. gloss of "raising their self-esteem"

    (b) They are respected and highly regarded.

23. • Full explanation of the metaphor
    • Sums up passage
    • negative connotation/effect of celebrity worship

English Foundation Level
Reading 2006

1. In the valley of Yosemite National Park

2. stares/intently/stares intently

3. She is looking through/has a telescope

4. steep/high/big, frightening

5. *Any three of*:
   sensation/calmly/quickly/methodically/comfortable/scaling

6. *Any two of*:
   reference to Scott being high up
   reference to skyscraper being high/tall
   reference to American setting

7. (i) climb is particularly difficult or dangerous/near vertical/high altitude

   (ii) few hand and foot holds/no Americans have climbed it before

8. (a) *Any three of*:
   sponsorship clothing deal/own agent/media coverage/female fans

   (b) title/name magazine

9. (i) youngest person to climb the nose (of) El Capitan

   (ii) youngest person to do the climb in one day

10. dedication

11. It's an American spelling/what Scott calls her/American way of referring to mother

12. Sends back pizza/refuses to eat things or is fussy

13. were around five/very few, now over 500

14. (Scott) bounds through the glass doors/nods hello

15. (a) his feet are a much bigger size

    (b) his feet are more sensitive

16. (a) • His rope looks like a spider's thread
    • He uses his arms and legs at full stretch
    • He holds his body at the same angle as the wall

    (b) dangling (in the air)

17. measly existence/just get by

18. *Any two of*:
    • in the gym for three hours
    • tried the same route five times
    • staying there until he gets it right

19. (a) any positive impression, e.g. dedicated/skilful/popular/ordinary
    negative impression (e.g. arrogant/obsessive) is also acceptable

    (b) Any two relevant quotes or pieces of textual evidence linked to your answer for 19 (a)

English General Level
Reading 2006

1. (a) (narrator's) maths teacher

   (b) her face reminds him of/looks like the moon

2. • to show or emphasise or highlight its
     importance
   • to contrast with the list of negatives in
     paragraph 1

3. boredom/boring/not interested

4. uses simile/comparison: chalk to dagger

5. (i) talking rubbish/nonsense

   (ii) speaking very fast/out of control

6. • build up/increase/sustain
   • tension/drama/curiosity

7. (a) He feels isolated
       He is suffering

   (b) Lonely and tormenting

8. repetition of "no"
   OR lists: no trees... no huts, no hills, no beaches/
   what is not there
   OR reference to long sentence followed by short
   sentence; reference to position of "only doubt"

9. (a) "I would love to go on a date with you, but I'm
       afraid I have to change my cat's litter box that
       night"
       OR
       "Oh, John, do you exist?" / "Are you here on
       earth with me?" / "I wasn't aware we were
       sharing the same universe."

   (b) suggests an unpleasant task preferable to a date
       with him
       OR
       ridiculous comment for someone in the same
       class

10. • pen shook
    • trembling hand
    • damp hand

11. • monumental
    • fateful

12. He wants Gloria/to encourage Gloria to tick the
    larger/the yes box

13. she won't be alone after maths
    OR
    if he doesn't act now she might go out with
    someone else

14. reference to countdown
    OR
    "Only ten minutes left... seven minutes left... six
    minutes left... Now there are five"

15. (to show/suggest) how desperate he is
    OR
    Inside (his head) he is shouting

16. (a) Any one of:
        short sentences/short
        paragraphs/simile/onomatopoeia/metaphor/
        hyperbole/exaggeration/exclamation marks

    (b) full explanation linked to growing excitement

17. *Any three of*:
    • her back is to the class
    • exchange takes place quickly
    • note passed very slowly/under the desk
    • hand returns very quickly

18. He feels he will now understand any of her
    reactions.

19. *Any two of*:
    • short sentence
    • humorous
    • surprise ending / reader does not expect her
      to eat it

20. *Any two of*:
    Realistic
    possible reasons:
    • passing notes/doing things without the
      teacher noticing
    • boring teacher/pupil not interested
    • being nervous about/asking someone out
    • use of nicknames
    Unrealistic
    possible reasons:
    • narrator's version of events is too exaggerated

English Foundation Level
Reading 2007

1. (a) bounding

   (b) (Once) abandoned

2. not being fast enough (on the track)

3.

exciting	
true	
fictional	
moving	✓

4. had to select one (dog) more than 100/many to choose from

5. *Any three from:*
   - (correct) colouring
   - reaction to sound is fine
   - had to be entire dog
   - obedient
   - compatible/good with other animals
   - compatible/good with people
   - couldn't be anything wrong with him

6.

	True	False	Cannot Tell
Sue trained Celt in Northern Ireland.		✓	
Celt spent more time being filmed than being trained.	✓		
Celt did well on the film set.	✓		
Sue Potter owns two cats.			✓

7. to separate/introduce/indicate pause before/ highlight the importance of the question

8. (thoroughly) pampered/(after) all the attention (he had received)

9. *Any three from:*
   - Chairman of Dogs Trust
   - had owned a rescued dog
   - his own greyhound had died
   - ref. to 500 acres open hills and farmland/lots of space
   - ref. to other pets

10. to provide education because they are out of school
    OR
    to help/improve their acting

11. (a) greyhounds well known for chasing small/furry animals which they mistake for the hare (on the track)

    (b) *Any two from:*
    - ref. to use of alliteration/repetition
    - word choice
    - exaggeration

    (c)
    - Yes: shows how much he liked cats (or similar idea)

    - No: ref. to fact it's only an animal/not a real tragedy (or similar idea)

12.

long-lasting	
short-term	✓
animal	
caring	

13. *Any two from:*
    - ref. to other dogs
    - sat on every chair he could
    - wanted to jump on the bed

14.
    - don't need a lot of exercise
    - like (sitting in an armchair) watching TV

15. use of list

16.
    - father said no
    - was moving house

17.
    - ref. to Celt having a nice home/things turning out well for Celt

    - "lucky" alone

18.

Film students	
Vets	
General readers	✓
Dog breeders	

19. *Any two from:*
    - ref. to alliteration
    - ref. to it summarises Celt's experiences
    - ref. to explanation of contrast between 'dumped' and 'lucky'

English General Level
Reading 2007

1. fed up (or similar) with her current job

2. says it sounds fun when it is dangerous/people try to stop themselves getting killed

3. not relevant for what she wanted to do/don't need academic qualifications to be a wall of death rider

4. (a) fantastic/unbelievable/the best

   (b) short sentences/minor sentences

5. *Any two from:*
   - gloss of 'skeletal', e.g. very basic or lightweight structure/frame of vehicle
   - gloss of 'driving . . . within six inches of the safety wire', e.g. getting very close to the audience
   - gloss of '20 shows a day', e.g. so many performances

6. attract/speak to/excite crowd/audience

7. - suggests coins *falling down* into the ring
   - suggests *a lot/number* of coins

8. to encourage donations/money

9. *Any two from:*
   - ref. to speed
   - ref. to nature of movement
   - ref. to expertise

10. ref. to number in the past, ref. to number in the present, e.g. almost 30 in the 1930s and 1940s, now only four

11. troupe

12. *Any two from:*
    suggest ground is wet (after winter), ref. to onomatopoeia, ref. to discomfort

13. long (sentence), list of activities/verbs

14. straight, no/few knots

15. *Any two from:*
    - keep going when the rider does not touch the throttle
    - driven by left hand only
    - don't fall over

16.

Technique	Evidence
comparison informal tone	ref. to modern bikes cops/zoom around/to your heart's content
use of second person	Take your hand/you can zoom/to your heart's content . . .
repetition	Take your hand/round/your
use of illustration	Chicago cops . . .

17. Tornado suggests speed/idea of going round and round/danger/power.
    Black Baron suggests mystery/death/menace/use of alliteration linked to catchy name (or similar).

18. (a) *Any four from:*
    - ref. to lions
    - ref. to roller skates
    - ref. to skeleton
    - ref. to cutting engine
    - ref. to flames

    (b) *Any two from:*
    - need for more spectacular tricks (gloss of "had to have one stunt better than the other")
    - competition from neighbouring attractions (gloss of "competing side by side")
    - to thrill/scare spectators (gloss of "causing the audience to gasp")
    - to exaggerate the danger

19. (a) wrongly applied name

    (b) no fatal accidents (on British walls)

20. technical term/name used by (or quote from) riders

21. *Any three from:*
    - ref. to Luke's (total) dedication
    - ref. to Luke and Kerri's 'partnership'
    - ref. to young Alex 'raring for his first go'
    - ref. to spieler giving up his job

22. *Any two from:*
    - single sentence for greater impact
    - ref. to Kerri is a link to the opening paragraphs
    - clearly shows writer's admiration for Kerri
    - sums up commitment of all involved

English Writing - 2008 (Cont.)

5 : 6   Grade 5 may have positive features such as a runaway enthusiasm which may detract the stated purpose but it will present the **gist** of the experience without **ramblings** and incoherence which, along with **numerous errors** and near-illegible handwriting are the mark of Grade 6.

Free Choice Numbers 14, 17.

Task specification/rubric/purposes

This question calls for the candidate to determine the purpose of the writing and format. It is, therefore, important that the candidate's writing purpose is made clear in the course of the response. Markers should assess according to the appropriate criteria.

No 14   the rubric restricts the candidate to the use of the picture and its associated ideas.

No 17   the rubric restricts the candidate to the use of the picture and its associated ideas.

No 18 imposed format of informative article for school magazine. The purpose here, however, is W1 to convey information. Some latitude may be required in terms of the degree/extent of the anecdotal/personal. This, too, may influence the tone but is acceptable as it is within the parameters of the rubric.

No 19 agree/disagree or balanced view. Personal/anecdotal evidence is very likely to feature in responses to this rubric.

No 21 agree/disagree or balanced. Both facets of education must be covered (inside and outside). A clear line of thought/argument should be presented with supporting evidence. Anecdotal evidence is, again, likely to feature but should be used to pursue a line of thought.

Grade Differentiation – Discursive

1 : 2 Grade 1 responses will show a **combination of depth**, **complexity and skilful deployment** of ideas, and will also marshall evidence in support of an argument.

Grade 2 responses will lack this combination of technical skill and confident tone, presenting ideas in a **less developed** or **sustained** manner.

3 : 4 Grade 3 will attempt an orderly flow of ideas, which may not succeed logically, whereas Grade 4 will be typically **weak in structure**, or **have thin ideas** or poorly constructed sentences.

5 : 6 Grade 5 will present ideas and opinions in **concrete**, **personal terms** which may be anecdotal, but are more than a bald series of unsupported, **disjointed** or **rambling** statements, the hallmarks of Grade 6.

Grade Differentiation – Informative

1 : 2 Grade 1 will convey information in a **clear sequence**, **selecting and highlighting** what is most significant. Grade 2 responses will be **less well sustained** in terms of the qualities of distinction in **ideas**, **construction and language**.

3 : 4 Grade 3 will convey the relevant information **in some kind of sequence** which may not succeed logically, whereas Grade 4 will be **weak in structure** or have **thin ideas** or **weak sentence construction**.

5 : 6 Grade 5 will convey only **simple information**. Formal errors will be obtrusive but the writing will not be marked by the **rambling** and **disjointed** statements which define Grade 6.

Personal Experience/Descriptive Numbers 3, 4, 6, 8, 11, 22.

Task specifications/rubric/purposes

Each of the above calls for a personal response; while there are no genre requirements here, content must be specific and appropriate.

No 3 a single occasion is required. The idea of both the 'journey' and the 'unexpected' should be presented although some latitude should be allowed with the latter. Associated thoughts and feelings should be rendered.

No 4 some latitude is required here. There may be some overlaps across W1 (conveying information) and W3 (conveying feelings and reactions) and possibly even W2 (deploying ideas).

No 6 the rubric restricts the candidate to a single occasion, although a number of scenes may be used to progress the idea of tested loyalty.

No 8 a single occasion is required. The nature of the 'authority' should be interpreted liberally. The evocation of both thoughts and feelings is an explicit requirement of the rubric.

No 11 a single occasion is required. The idea of the value of the lesson is clearly very open. The lesson, however, must be learned from 'an older relative.' Again, thoughts and feelings should be expressed.

No 22 description of a scene is an explicit requirement of the rubric. Candidates should choose ONE of the two options.

Grade Differentiation

1 : 2 Grade 1 will be a well crafted, stylish account and will deploy a range of skills to express perceptiveness and self-awareness and to achieve or create effects, while a Grade 2 account will be soundly constructed and show a **measure of insight** and self-awareness expressed accurately. Grade 2 may not be succinct but will be **substantial**.

3 : 4 A Grade 3 response will be reasonably well sustained, with easily grasped structure, and will on the whole be correct but with a certain dull monotony.

Grade 4 will be structurally weak and thin in ideas but will still attempt involvement, **approaching the overall adequacy** of Grade 3.

English Writing – 2008

Narrative Numbers 1, 7, 9, 12, 16, 20.

Task specifications/rubric/purposes

The criteria demand appropriate ideas and evidence of structure which in the narrative genre involve **plot** or **content** or **atmosphere**.

Note that the development of setting and character as well as plot is an explicit requirement for all of the short story options.

No 1   short story   imposed opening should be continued.

No 7   short story   imposed title **The School Gate** should be reflected in the narrative.

No 9   short story   choice of imposed titles from which the candidates must select ONE from either **Seeing is Believing** or **Close Up**. Title selected must be reflected in the narrative.

No 12   short story   imposed opening should be continued.

No 16   short story   choice of imposed title from which candidates must select ONE from either **A New Beginning** or **Touchdown**. Title selected must be reflected in the narrative.

No 20   short story   imposed opening should be continued.

Grade Differentiation

1 : 2   Grade 1 narrative will show **overall distinction** in IDEAS, CONSTRUCTION and LANGUAGE, and will be both **stylish and skilful**, while Grade 2 narrative will fall short both in the quality and in the **combination** of skills.

3 : 4   Grade 3 responses will have an **appropriate plot**, will make use of appropriate **register** to create ATMOSPHERE or SUSPENSE and should include NARRATIVE or DESCRIPTIVE details to establish the main lines of the plot. Do not forget that lack of variety in plot and language skills is typical of Grade 3. Accuracy is the criterion to establish here.

Grade 4's **simple plot** will approach the adequacy of Grade 3 but may be poorly organised or have significant inaccuracies.

5 : 6   Grade 5's **very basic plot** will occasionally try to achieve particular effects, and it will also be poorly organised and have significant inaccuracies.

Grade 6 will have a combination of negative features, will be **rambling**, or have **obscurities** in the plot and the marker will have difficulty in decoding because of very poor spelling, sentencing, or handwriting.

NB   If candidates ignore the rubric in respect of plot or character this may place them in Grade 5 in terms of purpose ('few signs of appropriateness'), unless there are other strong compensating features ('accurate', 'varied', 'sensitive'). Where there are no strong compensating features, this may tip the balance overall into Grade 6.

Discursive/Informative Numbers 2, 5, 10, 13, 15, 18, 19, 21.

Task specifications/rubrics/purposes

The rubrics cover controversial issues which are likely to elicit emotional responses. Objectivity is not required but clear, straightforward presentation of a point of view is required. At all levels, candidates must deal with the specific topics or, as is the case in one of the tasks, use the imposed format to convey information about a specific activity.

No 2   agree/disagree or balanced view. Candidates may choose to deal with the topic from one particular point of view or take a more balanced approach to the topic. Some background knowledge is required. Personal/anecdotal evidence may figure but should be used to support the candidate's argument.

No 5   agree/disagree/balanced view. Personal or anecdotal evidence may very well feature but should follow a line of thought.

No 10   agree/disagree/balanced view. Personal or anecdotal evidence may well feature but should pursue a line of thought.

No 13   agree/disagree/balanced. Personal/anecdotal evidence may be present but this should pursue a line of thought.

No 15   agree/disagree/balanced view. Some background knowledge is required. Personal/anecdotal evidence is likely to be used but it should reinforce the argument.

No 16 a single occasion is required. The 'duty' should be 'unpleasant' but allow some degree of latitude here. The expression of associated thoughts and feelings is an explicit requirement of the rubric.

No 20 description of scene is an explicit requirement.

No 22 this is mainly a personal piece of writing but it may include opinions. ONE such 'special' occasion should be selected and described. The idea of 'celebration' should be present and, again, interpreted liberally. The significance of the event to not only the candidate but also to his/her family and community should be stated. There may be an imbalance in the response with a **focus** on one particular area. This is acceptable given the demands of both time and the rubric.

Grade Differentiation

1 : 2 Grade 1 will be a well crafted, stylish account and will deploy a range of skills to express perceptiveness and self-awareness and to achieve or create effects, while a Grade 2 account will be soundly constructed and show a **measure of insight** and self-awareness expressed accurately. Grade 2 may not be succinct but will be **substantial**.

3 : 4 A Grade 3 response will be reasonably well sustained, with easily grasped structure, and will on the whole be correct but with a certain dull monotony.

Grade 4 will be structurally weak or thin in ideas but will still **attempt involvement, approaching the overall adequacy** of Grade 3.

5 : 6 Grade 5 may have positive features such as a runaway enthusiasm which may detract from the stated purpose but it will present the **gist** of the experience without **ramblings** and **incoherence** which, along with **numerous errors** and near-illegible handwriting are the markers of Grade 6.

Free Choice Number 8

Task specification/rubric/purposes

This question calls for the candidate to determine the purpose of the writing and format. It is, therefore, important that the candidate's writing purpose is made clear in the course of the response. Markers should assess according to the appropriate criteria.

No 8 the rubric restricts the candidate to the use of the picture and its associated ideas.

English Writing - 2007 (Cont.)

No 14   agree/disagree/balanced. Personal/anecdotal evidence may be present but this should follow a line of thought.

No 15   agree/disagree/balanced view. Personal/anecdotal evidence is very likely to be used but it should reinforce a line of argument.

No 17   agree/disagree or balanced. Again, personal/anecdotal evidence may very well feature because of the nature of the question but this should be used to support the line of thought adopted by the candidate.

No 19   agree/disagree/balanced view. Some background knowledge is required.

No 21   agree/disagree/balanced. Imposed format of newspaper article. A clear line of thought/argument should be present with supporting evidence. Anecdotal evidence is, again, likely to feature but should be used to pursue a line of thought.

Grade Differentiation - Discursive

1 : 2   Grade 1 responses will show a **combination of depth**, **complexity and skilful deployment** of ideas, and will also marshall evidence in support of an argument.

Grade 2 responses will lack this combination of technical skill and confident tone, presenting ideas in a **less developed** or **sustained** manner.

3 : 4   Grade 3 will attempt an orderly flow of ideas, which may not succeed logically, whereas Grade 4 will be typically **weak in structure**, or **have thin ideas** or poorly constructed sentences.

5 : 6   Grade 5 will present ideas and opinions in **concrete**, **personal terms** which may be anecdotal, but are more than a bald series of unsupported, **disjointed** or **rambling** statements, the hallmarks of Grade 6.

Grade Differentiation - Informative

1 : 2   Grade 1 will convey information in a **clear sequence**, **selecting and highlighting** what is most significant. Grade 2 responses will be **less well sustained** in terms of the qualities of distinction in **ideas, construction and language**.

3 : 4   Grade 3 will convey the relevant information **in some kind of sequence** which may not succeed logically, whereas Grade 4 will be **weak in structure** or have **thin ideas** or **weak sentence construction**.

5 : 6   Grade 5 will convey only **simple information**. Formal errors will be obtrusive but the writing will not be marked by the **rambling** and disjointed **statements** which define Grade 6.

Personal Experience/Descriptive Numbers 1, 4, 7, 9, 11, 13, 16, 20, 22.

Task specifications/rubric/purposes

Each of the above calls for a personal response; while there are no genre requirements here, content must be specific and appropriate.

No 1   any ONE piece of technology is acceptable. The importance of this should be stressed. Opinions may be present and this is entirely acceptable.

No 4   some latitude is required here. There may be some overlaps across person, place and incident although candidates should make the focus clear.

No 7   the rubric restricts the candidate to a single special place and how it inspired. Description of the place may feature but is not a pre-requisite.

No 9   candidates must write about a single occasion although this may spread over time. The idea of being alone should be included and the positive feelings of happiness.

No 11   the rubric restricts to a single occasion although, again, this may be spread over time. The nature of the 'personal pressure' should be clear and the way(s) in which it was faced.

No 13   a single occasion is required. Candidates should concentrate not only on the narrative aspect but also on the associated thoughts and feelings. The nature of 'injustice' (which should be interpreted liberally) and the form of the 'stand' should be clearly delineated.

English Writing – 2007

Narrative Numbers 3, 5, 12, 18, 23.

Task specifications/rubric/purposes

The criteria demand appropriate ideas and evidence of structure which in the narrative genre involve **plot** or **content** or **atmosphere**.

>   Note that the development of setting and character as well as plot is an explicit requirement for all of the short story options with the exception of No 5, where it is implicit.

No 3 short story – choice of imposed titles from which the candidates must select ONE from either **Futureshock** or **She Saw the Future**. Title selected must be reflected in the narrative.

No 5 short story – imposed opening should be continued.

No 12 short story – choice of imposed titles from which the candidates must select ONE from either **The Underdog** or **Free at Last**. Title selected must be reflected in the narrative.

No 18 short story – choice of imposed titles from which the candidates must select ONE from either **Stranger in a Strange Land** or **No Return**. Title selected must be reflected in the narrative.

No 23 short story – imposed title **The Traveller** must be reflected in the narrative.

Grade Differentiation

1 : 2 Grade 1 narrative will show **overall distinction** in IDEAS, CONSTRUCTION and LANGUAGE, and will be both **stylish and skilful**, while Grade 2 narrative will fall short both in the quality and in the **combination** of skills.

3 : 4 Grade 3 responses will have an **appropriate plot**, will make use of appropriate register to create ATMOSPHERE or SUSPENSE and should include NARRATIVE or DESCRIPTIVE details to establish the main lines of the plot. Do not forget that lack of variety in plot and language skills is typical of Grade 3. Accuracy is the criterion to establish here.

Grade 4's **simple plot** will approach the adequacy of Grade 3 but may be poorly organised or have significant inaccuracies.

5 : 6 Grade 5's **very basic plot** will occasionally try to achieve particular effects, and it will also be poorly organised and have significant inaccuracies.

Grade 6 will have a combination of negative features, will be **rambling**, or have **obscurities** in the plot and the marker will have difficulty in decoding because of very poor spelling, sentencing, or handwriting.

NB If candidates ignore the rubric in respect of plot or character this may place them in Grade 5 in terms of purpose ('few signs of appropriateness'), unless there are other strong compensating features ('accurate', 'varied', 'sensitive'). Where there are no strong compensating features, this may tip the balance overall into Grade 6.

Discursive/Informative Numbers 2, 6, 10, 14, 15, 17, 19, 21

Task specifications/rubrics/purposes

The rubrics cover controversial issues which are likely to elicit emotional responses. Objectivity is not required but clear, straightforward presentation of a point of view is required. At all levels, candidates must deal with the specific topics or, as is the case in one of the tasks, use the imposed format to convey information about a specific activity.

No 2 agree/disagree or balanced view. Candidates may choose to deal with the topic from one particular point of view or take a more balanced approach to the topic. Some background knowledge is required. Personal/anecdotal evidence may figure but should be used to support the candidate's line of argument.

No 6 agree/disagree/balanced view. Personal/anecdotal evidence may feature but should follow a line of thought.

No 10 imposed format of informative article for travel magazine. The purpose here, however, is to convey information. Some latitude may be required in terms of the degree/extent of the anecdotal/personal. This too may influence the tone but this is acceptable as it is within the parameters of the title.

English Writing - 2006 (Cont.)

Grade Differentiation

1 : 2   Grade 1 will be a well crafted, stylish account and will deploy a range of skills to express perceptiveness and self-awareness and to achieve or create effects, while a Grade 2 account will be soundly constructed and show a **measure of insight** and self-awareness expressed accurately. Grade 2 may not be succinct but will be **substantial**.

3 : 4   A Grade 3 response will be reasonably well sustained, with easily grasped structure, and will on the whole be correct but with a certain dull monotony.

Grade 4 will be structurally weak and thin in ideas but will still **attempt involvement, approaching the overall adequacy** of Grade 3.

5 : 6   Grade 5 may have positive features such as a runaway enthusiasm which may detract from the stated purpose but it will present the **gist** of the experience without **ramblings** and **incoherence** which, along with **numerous errors** and near-illegible handwriting are the markers of Grade 6.

Free Choice Number 4

Task specifications/rubric/purposes

This task calls for the candidate to determine the purpose of the writing and format. It is, therefore, important that the candidate's writing purpose is made clear in the course of the response. Markers should assess according to the appropriate criteria.

No 4   the rubric restricts the candidate to the use of the picture and its associated ideas as the stimulus for the writing piece.

No 15 **agree/disagree/balanced view of the issue**. Candidates should follow a line of argument with supporting evidence. Some candidates may base their argument on anecdotal evidence but this should follow a line of thought.

No 17 **agree/disagree/balanced**. Some background knowledge is required. Personal/anecdotal evidence may be present but this should follow a line of thought.

No 20 **agree/disagree/balanced view**. Candidates should indicate the reasons behind their opinions.

No 7 the main purpose is to convey information in the form of a newspaper report.

Grade Differentiation – Discursive

1 : 2 Grade 1 responses will show a **combination of depth, complexity** and **skilful deployment** of ideas, and will marshall evidence in support of an argument.

Grade 2 responses will lack this combination of technical skill and confident tone, presenting ideas in a **less developed** or **sustained manner.**

3 : 4 Grade 3 will attempt an orderly flow of ideas, which may not succeed logically, whereas Grade 4 will be typically **weak in structure**, or **have thin ideas** or poorly constructed sentences.

5 : 6 Grade 5 will present ideas and opinions in **concrete, personal terms** which may be anecdotal, but are more than a bald series of unsupported **disjointed** or **rambling statements**, the hallmarks of Grade 6.

Grade Differentiation – Informative

1 : 2 Grade 1 will convey information in a **clear sequence, selecting and highlighting** what is most significant. Grade 2 responses will be **less well sustained** in terms of the qualities of distinction in **ideas, construction and language.**

3 : 4 Grade 3 will convey the relevant information **in some kind of sequence** which may not succeed logically, whereas Grade 4 will be **weak in structure** or have **thin ideas** or **weak sentence construction.**

5 : 6 Grade 5 will convey only **simple information.** Formal errors will be obtrusive but the writing will not be marked by the **rambling** and **disjointed** statements which define Grade 6.

Personal Experience/Descriptive Numbers 1, 5, 9, 11, 12, 13, 18.

Task specifications/rubric/purposes

Each of the above calls for a personal response; while there are no genre requirements here, content must be specific and appropriate.

No 1 a single incident should be selected by the candidates. Candidates should concentrate not only on the narrative but also on associated thoughts and feelings.

No 5 a storm should feature in the narrative and candidates must also convey the elements of both excitement and fear associated with the experience.

No 9 candidates should enjoy a degree of latitude here. The word, 'plans', for example, should be interpreted flexibly.

No 11 candidates must write about both the 'highs' and 'lows'. The magazine article format here is secondary to personal writing purpose.

No 12 a single occasion is required but the title allows for a wide range of responses to that occasion. The ideas of 'new people' and 'new surroundings' should both feature.

No 13 a single occasion is clearly required where there is a delay during a journey. Candidates should concentrate not only on the narrative aspect but also on the associated thoughts and feelings. These feelings may include emotions at the time or feelings on reflection.

No 18 a single occasion is required where the candidate felt that no one was listening. The focus is on associated thoughts and feelings, either at the time or on reflection.

English Writing – 2006

Narrative Numbers 2, 6, 10, 14, 16, 19, 21.

Task specifications/rubric/purposes

The criteria demand appropriate ideas and evidence of structure which in the narrative genre involve **plot** or **content** or **atmosphere**.

No 2   short story –   imposed title **Never Forgotten** must be reflected in the narrative.

No 6   short story –   Candidates must select ONE of the two options: either Stormchaser or Lightning Strikes Twice. The selection must be reflected in the narrative.

No 10   short story –   imposed title **The Examination** must be evident in the narrative.

No 14   short story –   imposed title **The Road to Nowhere** must be reflected in the narrative.

No 16   short story –   ONE of the TWO openings must be used. The selection must be reflected in the narrative.

No 19   short story opening – Candidates must clearly develop setting, characterisation, and plot.

No 21   short story –   imposed title **Out of Time** must be reflected in the narrative. Candidates must clearly develop setting, characterisation, and plot.

Grade Differentiation

1 : 2   Grade 1 narrative will show **overall distinction** in IDEAS, CONSTRUCTION and LANGUAGE, and will be both **stylish** and **skilful**, while Grade 2 narrative will fall short both in the quality and in the **combination** of skills.

3 : 4   Grade 3 responses will have an **appropriate plot**, will make use of appropriate **register** to create ATMOSPHERE or SUSPENSE and should include NARRATIVE or DESCRIPTIVE details to establish the main lines of the plot. Do not forget that lack of variety in plot and language skills is typical of Grade 3. Accuracy is the criterion to establish here.

        Grade 4's **simple plot** will approach the adequacy of Grade 3 but may be poorly organised or have significant inaccuracies.

5 : 6   Grade 5's **very basic plot** will occasionally try to achieve particular effects, and it will also be poorly organised and have significant inaccuracies.

        Grade 6 will have a combination of negative features, will be **rambling**, or have **obscurities** in the plot and the marker will have difficulty in decoding because of very poor spelling, sentencing, or handwriting.

        NB   If candidates ignore the rubric in respect of plot or character this may place them in Grade 5 in terms of purpose ('few signs of appropriateness'), unless there are other strong compensating features ('accurate', 'varied', 'sensitive'). Where there are no strong compensating features, this may tip the balance overall into Grade 6.

Discursive/Informative Numbers 3, 8, 15, 17, 20, 7

Task specifications/rubrics/purposes

The rubrics cover controversial issues which are likely to elicit emotional responses. Objectivity is not required but clear, straightforward presentation of a point of view is required. At all levels, candidates must deal with the specific topics.

No 3   **agree/disagree or balanced view**. Candidates may choose to deal with the topic from one particular point of view or take a more balanced approach to the topic. Personal/anecdotal evidence may figure but should be used to support the candidate's argument.

No 8   **agree/disagree/balanced view**. Personal/anecdotal evidence may figure but should support a line of thought.

English Writing—2006 to 2008

	Credit	General	Foundation
	The work displays some distinction in ideas, construction and language. This is shown by a detailed attention to the purposes of the writing task; by qualities such as knowledge, insight, imagination; and by development that is sustained. Vocabulary, paragraphing and sentence construction are accurate and varied.	The work shows a general awareness of the purposes of the writing task. It has a number of appropriate ideas and evidence of structure. Vocabulary is on the whole accurate, but lacks variety.	The work shows a few signs of appropriateness and commitment to the purposes of the writing task.
As the task requires the candidate can	convey information, selecting and highlighting what is most significant;	convey information in some kind of sequence;	convey simple information;
	marshall ideas and evidence in support of an argument; these ideas have depth and some complexity; he/she is capable of objectivity, generalisation and evaluation;	order and present ideas and opinions with an attempt at reasoning;	present ideas and opinions in concrete personal terms;
	give a succinct account of a personal experience: the writing has insight and self-awareness;	give a reasonably clear account of a personal experience with some sense of involvement;	convey the gist of a personal experience;
	express personal feelings and reactions sensitively;	express personal feelings and reactions with some attempt to go beyond bald statement;	make a bald statement of personal feelings or reactions;
	display some skills in using the conventions of a chosen literary form, and in manipulating language to achieve particular effects.	use some of the more obvious conventions of a chosen literary form, and occasionally use language to achieve particular effects.	display a rudimentary awareness of the more obvious conventions of a chosen literary form, and occasionally attempt to use language to achieve particular effects.

A combination of these qualities may be called for by any one writing task.

	Credit	General	Foundation
Intelligibility and Correctness	Writing which the candidate submits as finished work communicates meaning clearly at a first reading. Sentence construction is accurate and formal errors will not be significant.	Writing which the candidate submits as finished work communicates meaning at first reading. There are some lapses in punctuation, spelling and sentence construction.	Writing which the candidate submits as finished work communicates meaning largely at first reading: however, some further reading is necessary because of obtrusive formal errors and/or structural weaknesses, including inaccurate sentence construction and poor vocabulary.
Length	When it is appropriate to do so, the candidate can sustain the quality of writing at some length. Pieces of extended writing submitted in the folio of coursework should not normally exceed 800 words in length. The overriding consideration is, however, that the length should be appropriate to the purposes of the writing task.	Length is appropriate to the purposes of the writing task.	100 words is to be taken as a rough guide to the minimum length expected for each finished piece of work, but the overriding consideration should be that the length is appropriate to the purposes of the writing task.

	Grade 1	Grade 2	Grade 3	Grade 4	Grade 5	Grade 6
Differentiating Factors	The finished communication is not only clear; it is also stylish. Attention to purpose is not only detailed; it is also sensitive. Writing shows overall distinction in ideas, construction and language. Vocabulary is apt and extensive, and paragraphing and sentence construction are skilful. In these respects performance transcends the level of accuracy and variety acceptable at grade 2.	Evidence of one or more of the qualities of distinction in ideas, construction or language is present but these qualities are less well sustained and/or combined than at grade 1. In the main writing is substantial, accurate and relevant, but it lacks the insight, economy and style which characterises achievement at grade 1.	Writing is characterised by overall adequacy of communication. It conveys its meaning clearly and sentence construction and paragraphing are on the whole accurate. There is a reasonably sustained attention to purpose, and structure shows some coherence. Where appropriate there is a measure of generalisation and objectivity in reasoning.	Writing approaches the qualities of adequacy required for grade 3 but is clearly seen to be impaired in one of the following ways: there are significant inaccuracies in sentence construction or the work is thin in appropriate ideas or the work is weak in structure.	Writing rises a little above basic intelligibility and rudimentary attention to purpose. Formal errors and weaknesses are obtrusive but not as numerous as at grade 6. Attention to the purposes of the writing task is weak but the quality of the writer's ideas is perceptibly stronger than at grade 6.	Writing contains many formal errors and structural weaknesses but they do not overall have the effect of baffling the reader. The conveying of simple information is marked by obscurities and extraneous detail, and the presentation of ideas, opinions and personal experience is somewhat rambling and disjointed.

English General Level
Reading 2008

1. (a) (surfing) stickers

   (b) *Any two from:*
   • Thurso 23 miles away
   • have taken the right turn-off (for Thurso)
   • nearly at their destination

2. short paragraph/one sentence paragraph
   OR reference to word choice "big league" suggests
   dramatic or similar

3. (a) gloss of "tropical" eg hot/exotic/beach with
   palm trees

   (b) "raw"/"exposed"/"worst excesses of the
   Scottish climate"

4. the best (of all the Caithness surfing spots)

5. reference to speed/power/ferocity/frightening/
   danger/(rolling) movement/size/shape
   (Any two)

6. (i) (first time) held in Scotland

   (ii) furthest north it has been held

7. WCT   gloss of "premier division"
                eg best competitors/higher status

   WQS   gloss of "platform ... to move up
                into the big time" eg step towards
                the better competition
                accept reference to lower status

8. (i) reference to prize money

   (ii) (vital tour) points

9. (i) (enjoy) travelling/new place/adventure/new
   experience/

   (ii) one of the best waves in Europe/big reef break
   waves/

   (iii) reference to photographs
        (Any three)

10. cold/harsh conditions
    OR ref to "Thurso is one of the best waves in
    Europe, if not the world."

11. big/dramatic/exciting waves
    OR reference to challenging weather conditions OR
    ref to contrast with tropical events

12. they don't want/to protect from/to stop (or similar)
    overcrowding (or similar) lifts (0)

13. informal/chatty/slang or similar

14. (i) met surfers/addressed their concerns

    (ii) paid for car park improvements

15. "most of them are positive"
    must have whole expression

16. boycott

17. (a)

negative and angry	
quite pleased but worried	
excited and not really anxious	✓

   (b) *Any one from:*
   • "eagerly anticipating"
   • "makes me feel proud"
   • "don't think it's going to be that bad"
   • "doesn't anticipate a negative impact"
   • "it'll generate business for us"

18. (Thurso is) far away/unknown/like another world

19. (a) negative: gloss of "live out of your bag a lot" eg
    few comforts/few belongings with you/never in
    one place for long gloss of "long stints away
    from home" eg not at home for long periods of
    time

    (b) positive: reference to seeing many/varied/new
    places OR gloss of "perform well" eg
    (competition) success
    OR gloss of "get some really good waves" eg
    good conditions/exciting surf/waves just right

20. (i) length of ride

    (ii) difficulty of moves

    (iii) how they connect it all together

21. (i)

to tell the reader some amusing stories about surfing	
to inform the reader about a surfing competition in Scotland	✓
to argue against holding a surfing competition in Scotland	

    (ii) accept appropriate reference to information in
    the passage eg
    • surfing/the life of a surfer/the competition
    scoring system
    • Thurso as a surfing location/the WQS and
    WCT

English Foundation Level
Reading 2008

1. **when**: Christmas Eve
    where: (motorway) services/petrol station

2. (i) (nearly) five hours

    (ii) *Any two from:*
    - without (a sniff of) a lift
    - no one had (even) slowed down
    - weather was lousy
    - he'd dozed off
    (lift or gloss acceptable)

3. (i) (getting) dark

    (ii) fog (was coming in)

4. "drove by him"/"as if he wasn't there"

5. small/could fit under his legs

6. - it contained all he had
    - used to belong to his mum
    (lift or gloss acceptable)

7. (a) - to get a bed
        - something to eat

    (b) - (probably get) run over
        - reference to luck alone

8. (a) cough (1) had a cold for two months/a long time (1)

    (b) sleeping rough (1) for a year/a long time (1)

9. (i) warm up

    (ii) get cup of coffee

10. "presuming they'd serve him"/"he looked a mess"

11. (i) shivering (due to cold)
    (ii) wet through/ref. to jacket not keeping him dry
    (iii) puddles around his feet

12. not really shower-proof
    OR accept ref. to manufacturer's claim/
    advertising/written on jacket etc

13. (i) lights not on
    (ii) close to kerb

14. (a)

rhyme	
metaphor	
alliteration	
simile	✓

    (b) (i) he cannot see (clearly)
        (ii) helpless/cannot or does not move/
        afraid/stunned or similar

15. Billy cannot see him
    Ref. to deep voice/harsh voice

16. (i) driver is Scottish (like himself)/driver has Scottish accent (like his)

    (ii) driver can take him (all the way) home

17. Billy no longer feels that it is home/Billy is no longer sure that it is home/Billy uncertain about his reception or similar/Billy misses his home

18. ref. to cold/winter
    ref. to miserable/unwelcoming

19.

a conversation	
a gadget	
a way of behaving correctly	✓
a solution to a problem	

20. (i) silence

    (ii) brief responses

    (iii) *Any three from:*
    - interruption
    - does not want music
    - way he speaks
    - drives faster

21. he is not having a good time so he feels (even) worse/jealous
    OR if you are not having a good time you feel (even) worse
    (lift or gloss acceptable)

22. For "yes" accept any two suitable references such as:
    - homeless
    - unwell
    - no one to care for him
    - possibly in danger
    - afraid of Hank
    - hint of family problems
    - hardly any possessions
    - cold
    - wet

    For "no" accept any two suitable references such as:
    - he does get a lift at the end
    - he is going home
    - might have run away from home
    - possibly stole rucksack from mum